D1557581

Bit-Slice Design

Bit-Slice Design: Controllers and ALUs

Donnamaie E. White
Advanced Micro Devices, Inc.

Garland STPM Press
New York & London

Figures reproduced with the permission of *Advanced Micro Devices*.

15 14 13 12 11 10 9 8 7 6 5 4 3 2 1

Library of Congress Cataloging in Publication Data

White, Donnamaie E.   1942–
  Bit-slice design.

  Includes index.
  1. Bit slice microprocessors—Design and construction. I. Title.
TK7895.M5W49   621.3819'58'2   79-7465
ISBN 0-8240-7103-4

Published by Garland STPM Press
136 Madison Avenue, New York, New York 10016

Printed in the United States of America

__Contents__

v

_Preface

This text has been compiled from the current and highly popular Customer Education Seminar, ED2900A, "Introduction to the Am2900 Family," offered by Advanced Micro Devices. No attempt was made to duplicate all of the material presented in the customer seminar. The intent was instead to present a true "introduction" for the undergraduate hardware or software student that could be covered in one quarter or semester. The ED2900A seminar assumes that the attendee either has a background in assembly level programming or has a background in SSI/MSI design. This text also makes this assumption.

The flow is an orderly evolution of a CCU design, adding one functional block at a time. The material is presented in a dual approach, referring to both the hardware and the firmware, or the software impact, as each feature is discussed.

The controllers are presented first, followed by the RALUs and their support chips. Interrupts are presented in two sections broken down by the hardware evolution. The final chapter provides a "typical" configuration of an Am2900 state-machine architecture CPU.

Chapter 1 is an introduction to the reasons why microprogramming should be selected as the means of implementing a control unit. This chapter also presents a discussion of language interrelationships covering topics from the typing of the conventional programmer languages to the functioning of the hardware through the microprogram. The basic concept of what a control unit does is described using a primitive CCU (computer control unit). The 2900 Family is also introduced and this bipolar bit-slice family will be used throughout the text. The concepts, however, apply to *any* microprogrammable system.

Chapter 2 begins the design evolution of a controller and introduces timing considerations. The hardware-firmware duality of the design decisions are stressed. In relation to the CCU used as an example, the concept of a mapping PROM is introduced. Only PROMs are discussed, although DEMUX networks, gate arrays, and PLA (programmable logic array) and PLA-type logic units are often used to perform the decode operation. Microprogram memory (control memory) is also presented. PROMs are referred to throughout the text although ROMs, PROMs, EPROMs, WCS (writeable control storage), and even parts of main memory may serve as the control memory. Only single-level control memory is refered to in the text although some designs exist which use two-level control stores (nanoprogramming).

Chapter 3 continues the evolution of the controller adding subroutines, nested subroutines, loops, and case statements to the tools available to the microprogrammer. The concept of overlapping field definitions in a microinstruction is introduced in relation to the branch-address and counter-value fields. This is an elementary form of variable formatting, the use of which should be minimized for clarity. The controller evolution leads to the microprogrammable sequencers— the Am2909 and Am2911—and the next address control block, the Am29811. (The letters A or B following a chip identification refers to the latest version available and may vary over time.) The various versions are pin-compatible and differ usually in die size and speed.

The case statement introduces the Am29803A, a device which assists in implementing up to a 16-way branch.

Microprogram memory implementation is briefly discussed, introducing the use of the Am27S27 registered PROM, dc and ac loading, and the effects on sequencer timing of excessive capacitive load.

Chapter 4 continues the evolution of the CCU, introducing interrupt handling (the interrupt controller is discussed later). The interrupts are introduced here to demonstrate the $\overline{OE}_{VECT}$ requirement of the next address control block. The evolution finishes with a detailed discussion of the Am2910 instructions. The instructions are discussed in their conventional usage. A number of instruction set variations are possible by tying control lines to different instruction lines ($\overline{CCEN}$ to I_3, for example) and by ignoring the $\overline{PL}$, $\overline{VECT}$, and $\overline{MAP}$ outputs of the Am2910 and driving the output enables of these devices from the pipeline register (microinstruction) itself. The Am2914 interrupt controller is covered briefly.

Chapter 5 covers the RALUs—the Am2901 and Am2903—in a series of evolving steps as were the microsequencers. Every conceivable consideration cannot be discussed here, but enough is presented to cover the architecture of the Am2901.

Chapter 6 covers some basic operations and presents their microcodes to demonstrate microcode selection for these devices. Two's complement multiply is covered in-some detail to highlight the differences between the Am2901 and the Am2903.

Chapter 7 describes the ''typical'' CPU as suggested by Advanced Micro Devices for the ''typical'' user. It covers the Am29705 two-port RAM and the Am2904 ''LSI Glue'' multiplexer-register support chip.

An instructor's manual of exercises and solutions has been prepared and is available from Advanced Micro Devices.

Although the text is original, many of the drawings have appeared in application notes and data sheets previously published by Advanced Micro Devices and are reproduced with the permission of Advanced Micro Devices. Those application notes written by the Bipolar Applications Department have served as the principal reference material. Principal authors of these notes, to whom I am indebted for their assistance and advice are:

John Mick, Engineering Manager, Systems and Applications, Digital Bipolar Products.

the late Michael Economidis, Section Manager, Systems and Applications, Bipolar Memory and Programmable Logic, Mr. Economidis was an expert on the Am2914.

Jim Brick, Applications Engineer, Bipolar Microprocessors

Vernon Coleman, Senior Applications Engineer, Systems and Applications, Bipolar Microprocessor Circuit Definition.

William Harmon, Manager, Systems and Applications, Bipolar Microprocessing.

1

__ Introduction __

Over the years, there has been an evolution of the universal building blocks used by logic circuit designers. In the mid-1960s, there were SSI gates; NAND, NOR, EXOR, and NOT or INVERT. In the early 1970s, MSI blocks, registers, decoders, multiplexers, and others made their appearances. In the late 1970s, ALUs (arithmetic logic units) with on-board scratchpad registers, interrupt controllers, microprogram sequencers, ROMs/PROMs, and other LSI devices up to and including a complete one-chip microprocessor (control, ALU, and registers) became readily available.

SSI (small scale integration) is defined here to include chips containing approximately 2–10 gates. MSI (medium scale integration) is used for chips containing 20–100 gates. LSI (large scale integration) chips contain 200–1000 gates, with the upper limit continually extending as VLSI (very large scale integration) becomes a reality. The AmZ8000 CPU contains 17.5K gates; the M68,000 claims to contain 68,000 transistors.

Selection of the Implementation

Today, a designer is faced with three basic choices in implementation: (1) SSI/MSI hardwired logic; (2) 9080A/8080A (8-bit) or AmZ8000-In8086-M68000 (16-bit) MOS fixed instruction set (FIS) microproces-

1

sor; or (3) microprogrammable bit-slice architecture with the 2900 Family or other similar family. There are a number of factors which influence the decision as to which implementation is best for the application.

Architecture

In terms of the design architecture, any FIS MOS microprocessor by definition has its own predefined internal architecture, and this constrains the design options available. This fact is acceptable if the architecture provided by the selected MOS device satisfies the one desired for the application. An SSI/MSI implementation allows the designer to specify in complete, exact detail the architecture desired. With bit-slice devices, some constraints are placed on the designer, but most of the system architecture is left to user definition via the selected interconnections and the microprogram.

Size

The real estate or board space (rack space, etc.) is often of concern in a design because of space limitations. An FIS MOS microprocessor may use 3–6 chips for a typical average control system, versus 100–500 chips for the same system implemented in SSI/MSI and 30–60 chips for a compromise bit-slice design.

Word Length

The word length necessary for the system, whether a computer, controller, signal processor, or whatever, is usually known in advance. FIS MOS microprocessors can be used where their word length is compatible with the design objective. MOS devices exist for 4-, 8-, and 16-bit data word systems. Using SSI/MSI, any word length may be accommodated. Using bit-slice (the 2900 Family is expandable in multiples of 4 bits), a wide variety of useful word size systems are possible. When bit-slice does not conveniently match, SSI/MSI can be used to "patch" the basic bit-slice design.

Instruction Set

The instruction set that the system under design is to support has a major impact on the choice of implementation. The high dollar investment in software, which currently exceeds the hardware investments with a ratio as high as 10 to 1, often results in the prime directive of software compatibility: the new design *must* support the existing instruction set. FIS MOS microprocessors have a fixed instruction set. If there is an MOS microprocessor whose instruction set supports the design instruction set, then a microprocessor-based design can be used. The current FIS microprocessors support assembly level languages and have software to support BASIC, PL/1, FORTRAN, PASCAL, and even COBOL. If the design has an unusual instruction set requirement, it would require that a program written in the desired instruction set be passed through an additional software process prior to actual MOS device execution.

The two most widely known 16-bit devices are the In8086, with its 8080-based architecture and instruction set, and the AmZ8000, with a general-register architecture and an instruction set based on the IBM SYS/370 and the DEC PDP 11/45.

An SSI/MSI design can be customed tailored to support any desired instruction set. A bit-slice design can be microprogrammed to support any desired instruction set. The principal difference between these two approaches is that one is done exclusively in hardware and the other (bit-slice) is done in hardware and firmware.

Speed

Another design criterion or specification is the required speed of the design. SSI/MSI using Schottky TTL and bit-slice (2900 Family) can support systems with 125 ns cycle times. MOS microprocessors are slower, with approximate cycle times of 1–2 μs. The newer MOS devices support 4–5 MHz clock speeds. The newer bit-slice devices are targeted for 100 ns microcycle systems. When instruction times are given for an MOS microprocessor, the instruction is a machine level instruction. To properly compare this with bit-slice or SSI/MSI, *macro*instruction execution times must be used where a macroinstruction is a machine instruction which the microprogram supports. Bit-slice designs exist with effective macroinstruction times of 320 ns (HEX-29) and 200 ns (SUPER-16) for register–register operations (Chapters 8 and 9 of AMD's Bit-Slice Microprocessor Design Series).

Tradeoffs

Design tradeoffs are summarized in Table 1-1. Basically, where high speed, long word lengths, or critical instruction sets occur, MOS FIS cannot be used. If design time–parts count–board space restrictions also exist, or if production volume does not support the effort required to do an SSI/MSI design (considered the most difficult to do correctly), the bit-slice devices are the best choice. It should also be noted that a microprogrammed bit-slice design is upgraded or changed, usually through a change of PROM or a reload or patch of writable control store, more readily than is a hardwired SSI/MSI design.

Bit slice devices are applied to three basic areas: machines with long words, machines with special instruction sets, and high-speed

Table 1-1 Design Tradeoffs

	SSI/MSI	Bit-Slice Devices	FIS MOS Microprocessor
Architecture	Any Desired	Pseudoflexible	Predesigned
Physical size (typical)	500 chips	50	3–6
Word length	Any Desired	Multiples of 2, 4	4, 8, 16
Instruction set	Any desired; May be wired	Any desired may be microprogrammed	Constrained if speed a problem
Speed	100–200 ns	100–200 ns	1–2 μs
Design time	Long, slow, if done correctly	Fast	Fast
Debug	Difficult	Development systems aid process	Development systems aid process
Documentation	Tedious, often outdated	Forced via microprogram	Software is major portion
Upgrades	Up to a full redesign required	Easily done, can be preplanned	Easily done
Cost	Highest	Medium range	Lowest

machines. The best examples are signal processors, with a low volume per particular specification and which require high speed and a long data word, and emulators such as the one for the SIGMA 9 (32-bit word) and the one for the GE 400 (24-bit word), where software compatibility to the existing system at increased throughput is mandatory. Variable instruction set minicomputers have also been developed using bit-slice which allow custom-tailored instruction sets to be microprogrammed around one fixed hardware implementation.

Microprogramming

Microprogramming is to hardware design what structured programming is to software design. If a bipolar (Schottky TTL) machine is to be built, in bit-slice or in SSI/MSI, its control should be microprogrammed. First suggested by Wilkes as a methodical way of handling the control unit of a system, it is now recognized as the best approach. Why?

First, random sequential logic circuits are replaced by memory (writable control store or ROM [read-only memory] or PROM [programmable ROM] or related devices). This results in or forces a more structured organization on the design.

Second, when a unit is to be upgraded, a field engineer can replace the appropriate PROM considerably easier than hardwiring and patching new components onto a crowded printed circuit board (PCB) with all of the associated pitfalls of such activity.

Third, an initial design can be done such that several variations exist simply by substituting one or more PROMs (changing the microprogram), and enhanced versions can be preplanned such that version B is constructed by simply adding a PROM or two to version A, simplifying production. The basic units would contain sparsely populated PCBs with upgrades provided for in the etch and connections. In these cases, simply adding PROMs (and changing others as required) expands the system. This technique is also commonly used for RAM memory (read–write memory) expansion.

The microprogram, documented in the definition file and in the assembly source file, serves as the principle documentation of the firmware. This, coupled with the modularity of the design as enforced by the use of microprogram control, provides a better opportunity for clearer documentation than multipaged schematics can provide.

Last, diagnostic routines can be included in the PROMs supplied with the final system and can be called in by a field engineer through a test panel and executed to aid debug. Some diagnostic routines could be microprogrammed into the system such that they are routinely executed in the normal running environment. For more severe testing, the normal PROM memory could be swapped with a special test memory simply by substituting PROMs.

Advantages of LSI

If bipolar has been chosen over MOS because of speed, LSI is preferable to SSI/MSI for several reasons.

First, costs are reduced. LSI requires fewer parts and therefore fewer boards and less rack space. There is less etch and fewer pin connections with LSI as more and more of the connections are moved inside the package.

Second, using LSI improves reliability. Approximately 80% of the failures of working systems are caused by broken etch or by bent pins and other broken external connections. Using SSI/MSI, a typical controller might use 300 16-pin DIPs, for a total of 4800 pins. The same controller done with LSI might use 30 40-pin DIPs, for a 1200 pin total; the other connections having been moved inside of the package.

The 2900 Family is going to be introduced in this text. It is a design rule that every design should use industry-standard parts. The Am2900 family is considered to be the industry standard for bipolar bit-slice devices. It is a microprogrammable family of LSI-level complexity. Table 1-2 summarizes its advantages.

The Am2900 Family

The 2900 Family components include or will soon include (1) CPU-ALU and scratchpad register units: Am2901, Am2903, and the new Am29203; (2) microprogram sequencers and controllers: Am2909/2911 and Am2910; (3) bipolar memory: various devices, including error detection and correction controllers and support devices (Am2960 Series); (4) interrupt controller and support devices: Am2914, Am2913, and Am2902; (5) bus I/O: Am2950 and support devices; (6) DMA sup-

Table 1–2 Microprogramming with LSI—Advantages

More structured organization
Field changes—may be as simple as replacing a PROM
Adaptions—may be as simple as replacing a PROM
Expansions—preplanned, may be as simple as adding a PROM
Better documentation
Hardware and firmware can be designed in parallel
LSI uses fewer parts
LSI has better reliability
Diagnostic PROM can aid debug, maintenance

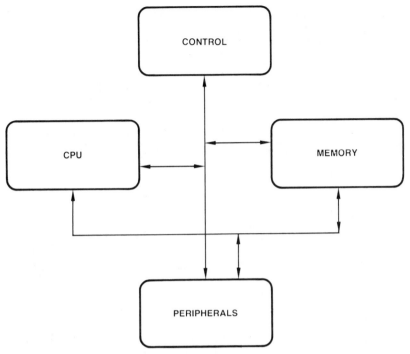

Figure 1-1.   Simplex system block diagram.

port: Am2940 and Am2942; (7) timing support via microprogrammable microcycles: Am2925; (8) main memory program control: Am2930 and Am2932; and (9) the new 16-bit Am29116.

Consider a simplex block diagram of a basic computer, shown in Figure 1-1. The essential blocks of this diagram are (1) the CPU (central processing unit), containing the ALU and scratchpad registers, the PC (program counter), and MAR (memory address register); (2) the main memory, where active programs and data are stored; (3) peripherals, including backup memory, input, and output; and (4) the CCU (computer control unit), which supervises everything else and contains the control logic instruction decode and the PROMs. The CPU is where data is processed; the CCU is where instructions are processed.

From this simple overview, progress to Figure 1-2 and the generalized computer architecture blocked out to show the various members of the 2900 Family and their applications.

Language Interrelationships

Programming classes relate source code—written by the user in some programming language—to object code—the machine level, machine-

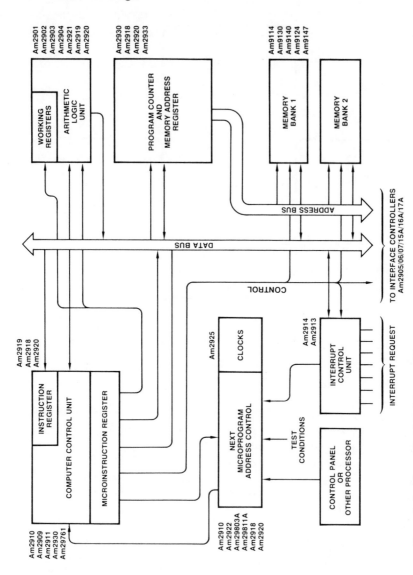

Figure 1–2. Generalized computer architecture.

executable instructions—via an assembler or compiler. A compiler is a software program that translates a high-level (compiler level) language program into object code. An assembler is a software program that translates an assembly level source program into object code. There are usually several compilers and one assembler per computer system.

Compilers translate at an average ratio of four to one (four machine instructions per source instruction [FORTRAN IV]) or higher (six to one for FORTRAN VI). Assemblers can be very nearly one to one, with assembly statements being a mnemonic form of the bit pattern machine instruction. In both cases, software is processed by software to produce software, as shown in Figure 1-3.

High-Level Language

High-level languages are fairly free format, i.e., they have few columnar placement restrictions on the coding form, use pseudo-English mnemonics, and have prewritten functions. Their capabilities include arrays, loops, branches, and subroutines, with the current emphasis on structured programming tools, such as IF-THEN-ELSE, CASE, and PROCEDURE statements.

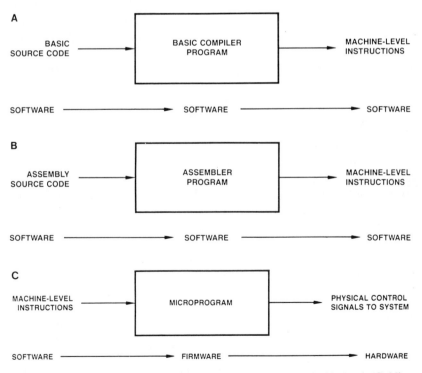

Figure 1–3.   Language relationships. (A) High level. (B) Assembly level. (C) Micro level.

Assembly Level Language

Assembly level languages have a more restricted format, require a precise data definition, may involve the programmer in program placement in memory, and use mnemonics for instructions but have more of them. Most instructions or statements are restricted to one operation—hence the approximate one to one translation ratio. The assembly level programmer in general must know more about the machine being used than the programmer who writes in FORTRAN or BASIC.

Machine Level Language

Machine level languages are the closest to the system of the software level languages. They are usually written using an encoding of instructions, data, and addresses in either octal or hexadecimal notation, are more tedious to construct and debug, and are more restrictive in the format required than the assembly level languages. They can require more specific detail from the programmer, depending on the complexity of the system being programmed.

Microprogramming

The machine level instructions are what the computer control unit (the CCU) receives. In a microprogrammed machine, each machine level instruction (referred to as a macroinstruction) is decoded and a microroutine is addressed which, as it executes, sends the required physical control signals in their proper sequence to the rest of the system. This is where the software instruction via a firmware microprogram is converted into hardware activity.

Microprogram Storage

The various software programs will vary from hour to hour, or more often, and their data will vary; therefore read–write or RAM memory is required as their storage area. The microprogram, however, will usually remain the same. There are a few machines—the Burroughs 1700, for example—that load a different microprogram for each of several application languages.

Where one microprogram is to be used by the system, ROMs (high production) or PROMs (lower production, prototype) are used for the microprogram memory. Such systems are called microprogrammed systems.

When a microprogram may be replaced by another, for example, to emulate another machine or to do a diagnostic run, then either a separate read–write memory, called a writable control store (WCS), or part of the system main memory is used as the microprogram memory with minifloppies, tape cartridges, or an area of main memory as the auxiliary storage for the microprograms. This alterability is attractive for special application systems such as experimentation control. Writable control storage is also useful for prototype systems and is present in development systems for flexibility. Systems with alterable microprograms are called microprogram*able* systems.

Throughout the remainder of the text, the microprogram control memory will be assumed to be a PROM memory for the sake of simplicity.

Format

Each machine level instruction is in the form of an op code and operands. There may be several different formats for the instructions in any one machine. These instructions are decoded by the control unit, and the decoding produces an address which is used to access the microprogram memory.

The microroutine for the individual machine or macroinstruction is called into execution and may be one or more microinstructions in length. (A microinstruction will be assumed to execute in one microcycle; such a microinstruction is also called a microstep.) Each microinstruction contains information blocked out in fields, where each microinstruction field directs or controls one or more specific hardware elements in the system. Every time that a particular machine instruction occurs the same microroutine is executed. The particular sequencing of the available microroutines constitutes the execution of a specific program.

Machine level language is very close to the hardware and has a very constrained format. It uses no mnemonics and requires that everything be specified by the programmer, including program address and data addresses. A sample machine instruction format is shown in Figure 1-4A. More than one machine instruction format usually exists for a given system.

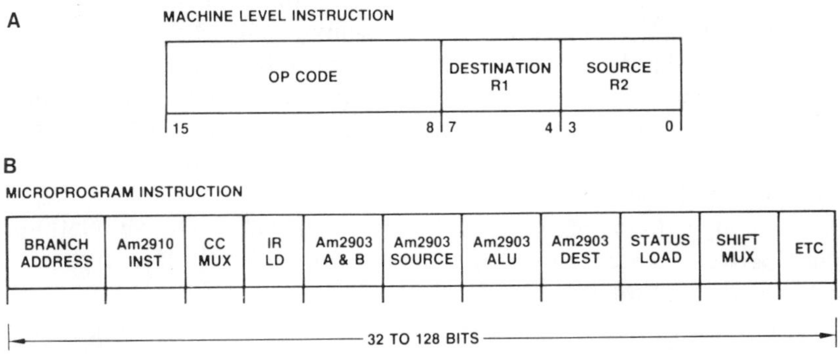

A   MACHINE LEVEL INSTRUCTION

OP CODE	DESTINATION R1	SOURCE R2
15	8 7 4	3 0

B
MICROPROGRAM INSTRUCTION

BRANCH ADDRESS	Am2910 INST	CC MUX	IR LD	Am2903 A & B	Am2903 SOURCE	Am2903 ALU	Am2903 DEST	STATUS LOAD	SHIFT MUX	ETC

──── 32 TO 128 BITS ────

Figure 1–4. Sample formats. (A) Sample machine level instruction (register addressing). (B) Sample microprogram instruction (Am2900 family). (Addr., address; CC, condition code test; Dest., destination; Inst., instruction; *n*, unknown number of bits; R1 and R2 are operands.)

Microprogramming is done in the format or formats *designed by the programmer*. Once chosen, it (or they) becomes fixed. Each field controls a specific hardware unit or units, and the possible bit patterns for each field are determined by the signals required by the hardware units controlled. Simple, short microprograms can be recorded in bit string fashion and prototype PROMs created using manually operated PROM burners. A sample microinstruction format is shown in Figure 1-4B. More than one microinstruction format may exist for a given microprogram.

Development Systems

Longer microprograms (> 32 microwords in length or with microwords > 16 bits wide) are better handled with development systems. These systems allow each field to be defined with mnemonics, which is a documentation aide. (Labels such as ON, OFF mean more to a human than 0, 1.) Once the fields are defined, the microcode (microprogram, microroutines, microinstructions) can be written in mnemonics, more or less as a pseudoassembly language, providing human-readable documentation in the process. The development system then may be used to assemble the microprogram thus written and to create the input to an automated PROM burner.

The development systems allow prototype hardware to be connected to them, and with the prototype microprogram loaded into the writable control store of the development system the development system can be used to debug hardware and firmware in parallel. The WCS is used to replace the microprogram control store of the prototype system. For the 2900 Family, the development system is Advanced Micro Computer's AmSYS 29™.

Microprogramming is the programming level that is closest to the hardware, and the microprogrammer must know everything about each of the pieces of hardware which are to be controlled. The tradeoff here is between the detail level of the programming and the power and the control of the hardware that is possible. The actual number of microroutines required is a function of the number of machine level instructions that the system is to recognize. For an average computer control system, there would be about four microinstructions per machine instruction, with the minimum being 1 and the maximum 16. This varies dramatically with the application. Figure 1-5 gives the relative relationships between the ease of programming and the level of control provided by each of the language levels.

Controller Design

A computer control unit (CCU) will be used for illustration throughout the text; the design approach, however, is applicable to *any* controller.

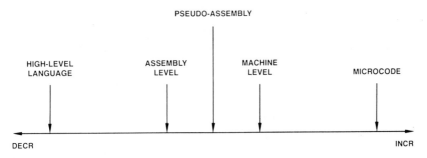

Figure 1–5. Language interrelationships: Requires (1) detailed knowledge of hardware; (2) time to write programs; (3) power and control of hardware.

A Simple Computer

The simplex computer of Figure 1-1 is further reduced as shown in Figure 1-6, which shows (1) a CCU, (2) the ALU and scratchpad registers, (3) the PC (program counter), and (4) MAR (memory address register).

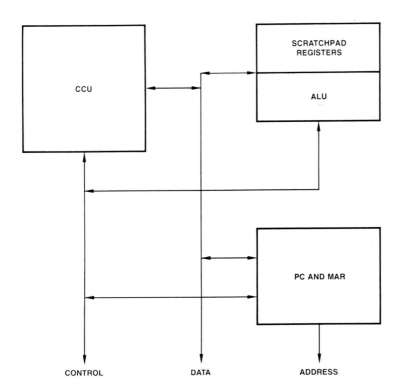

Figure 1–6. CPU and control block diagram.

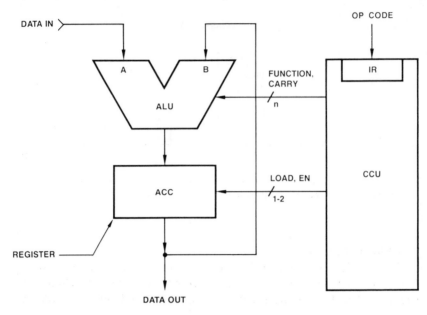

Figure 1–7. Simple sequential system (simple computer/SIMCOM).

The MAR is the output to the address bus for peripheral and memory addressing. The CCU controls all devices shown and outputs to external devices via the control bus. The ALU receives and outputs data via the data bus. Addresses may be loaded into the PC via the data bus. This is a very elementary system.

This system is reduced further in Figure 1-7, where the CCU is shown to control the ALU and the ACC (accumulator, a register) with its other control functions ignored for now. Here the data may be input only via port A of the ALU; port B is loaded via the ACC register; and data is output only from the ACC. The CCU receives an instruction in the form of an op code *somehow* (ignore how for the moment). Given the op code as input, the CCU must proceed to generate (1) the appropriate function control signals (three to six bits would be typical); (2) the ACC load-enable controls (two bits); and (3) the carry-in (C_{in}) bit value. For this elementary unit the microword format might appear as shown in Figure 1-8.

A simple ALU could have three control lines and perform addition, subtraction, and the logical OR, AND, EXOR, and similar functions, up to a total of eight functions. The carry-in bit allows the three arithmetic functions $A + B$, $A - B$, and $B - A$ to be varied to $A + B + 1$, $A - B - 1$, and $B - A - 1$. This simple ALU would support the machine level and assembly level instructions ADD, SUB, OR, AND, and EXOR, as shown in Figure 1-9.

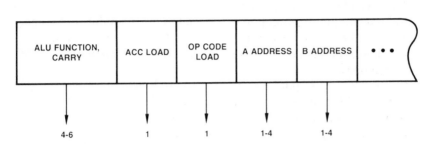

Figure 1–8. Control required from CCU.

Constructing the CCU

Now that what the CCU must do—namely, translate the op code received into ALU-ACC controls—is defined, how is the CCU constructed?

Hardwired Design

As stated before, the CCU can be built from the traditional sequential circuit network, an SSI/MSI hardwired unit. The advantages and justifications of this approach are as follows:

It is a custom design.
It may be a more minimal (irredundant, testable) solution.
It is justified if the design is to remain rigid or fixed.
It may be the highest-speed implementation.
It is justified if a high volume is to be produced before redesign.

CONTROL LINES			ALU FUNCTION	
S_2	S_1	S_0	$C_{IN} = 0$	$C_{IN} = 1$
0	0	0	A + B	A + B + 1
0	0	1	B–A–1	B–A
0	1	0	A–B–1	A–B
0	1	1	A∨B	
1	0	0	A∧B	
1	0	1	$\overline{A}$∧B	
1	1	0	A⊻B	
1	1	1	$\overline{A⊻B}$	

Figure 1–9. ALU functions.

The disadvantages are as follows:

There is a lengthy design time.

Documentation is difficult to create and to maintain due to volume.

Minimization to remove redundancy is difficult, if done at all.

If minimization is not done, redundancy will interfere with testability.

Design changes require a partial or total redesign.

Debug is difficult, with races or hazards.

Board space is high.

Pin count is high (external connections).

Modularity and therefore structure is usually not present.

A hardwired control would consist of and instruction register (IR), decode logic, a timing generator network, and a complex sequential-combinational network. Output from the network would be the control signals for the rest of the system, as shown in Figure 1-10.

Microprogrammed Design

Assuming that the required speed has negated using MOS FIS microprocessors, the control can be done with microprogramming.

The simplest microprogrammed computer control unit would require an instruction register, decode logic, a clock source, and a ROM- or PROM-based control memory. Output from the control memory would include the control signals for the rest of the system. If a control unit other than a CCU is being developed, the unit could be as simple as a register, a clock source, and a PROM-based control memory, as presented in Figure 1-11.

The advantages of a microprogrammed approach to the construction of a control unit are as follows:

It is custom design at a higher level.

Microprogramming allows a systematic approach to the design.

The result is a compact, modular physical unit (compared to SSI/MSI).

The result is a flexible design (the unit can be microprogrammed to perform different control functions and different variations of those functions, in most cases without affecting the physical hardware).

If a proper structured programming approach is used to create the microprogram, there will be better documentation of system operation than is possible with a hardware-only design.

Diagnostic routines could be microprogrammed into the control memory itself or into special PROMs for use in troubleshooting the system.

There is a shorter design time compared to SSI/MSI.

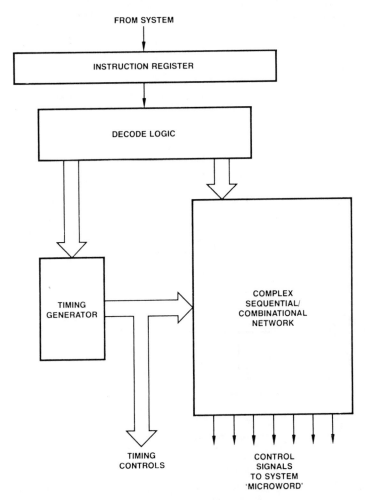

Figure 1–10.   Typical hardwired (SSI/MSI) CCU.

Design aids via development systems exist to support the above.

For a hardwired design, the design time goes up as people are added to a project above some critical number, such as two or three people. Microprogrammed design can use groups operating in parallel, since the microcode and hardware development can generally proceed in parallel.

Cost Effectiveness
The trend over time is for microprogramming to become the cost-effective method of control unit design at lower and lower levels of design complexity. The PDP-11 series of computers is a good example

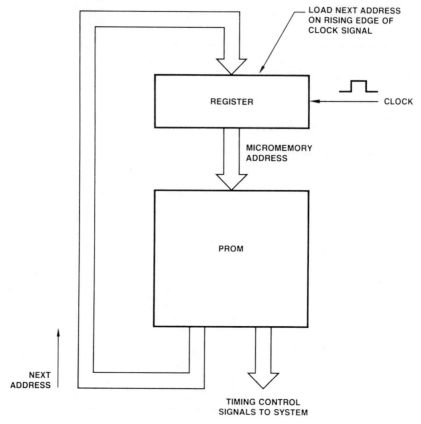

Figure 1–11.   Simplest control unit implementation. (Clock signal refers to the rising edge.)

of this trend. The PDP-11/20 was designed when hardwired logic was more cost effective for the level of "functionality" of the PDP-11; the PDP-11/60 was designed when microprogramming had become the more cost effective choice. The PDP-11/60 has more control functions implemented via microprogramming than does the PDP-11/20, although the "functionality" (design complexity) of the systems are considered to be approximately equal.

2

Simple
Controller

The very simplest microprogrammed controller is constructed from a PROM (assume that this means ROM *or* PROM from now on) and a register, as shown in Figure 2-1. The load enable on the register is connected to the clock signal. The register outputs an address to the PROM memory, and this address is used to fetch the next microinstruction that is to be executed. No next-address logic is included or required. After a time delay equal to that needed for stabilizing the register outputs plus the read access time of the memory, the memory outputs both the control signals to the rest of the system and the next address to be loaded into the register. The PROM memory is also referred to as the control memory. The output from the memory must be stable before the next clock pulse (C_p):

$$\underline{C}_p = \bar{t} \text{ read access} \quad + \bar{t} \text{ register} \quad + \bar{t} \text{ setup time}$$
$$\text{of memory} \qquad C_p \text{ to output} \qquad \text{for register}$$

The size of the memory is 2^n words, with each word M bits long. The M bits are formed from the C control bits plus the n address bits required to specifiy the next instruction:

$$M = C + n$$

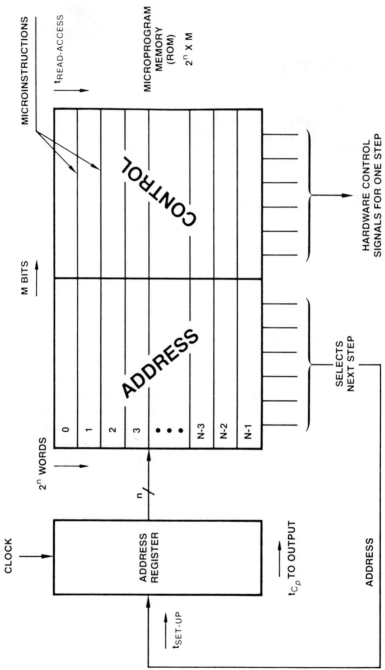

Figure 2–1.   The simplest implementation of a sequential machine.

word width equals the number of control bits plus the number of next-address bits.

The programmer is free to place microinstructions anywhere in any order as long as each one references the next executable address. This system will run from clock power up until clock power down. Assume on power up that the register is cleared and the first address executed is address 0. Since no next address logic is provided, only one sequence is possible. This controller is suitable for process control (repetitive looping of a sequence).

Sequential Execution

A reduction in required PROM memory is possible by removing the requirement of the next-address field. This is reasonable because the microprogram can be loaded into PROM in its executed order as one long sequential routine, as diagrammed in Figure 2-2. In this case the next microinstruction address is always equal to the current microinstruction address plus 1.

The register is replaced by a counter, incremented by the clock and reset to zero on startup. The clock pulse width is determined by

$$\underline{C}_p = \overline{t}_{\text{read access}} + \overline{t}_{\text{counter } C_p \text{ to output}}$$

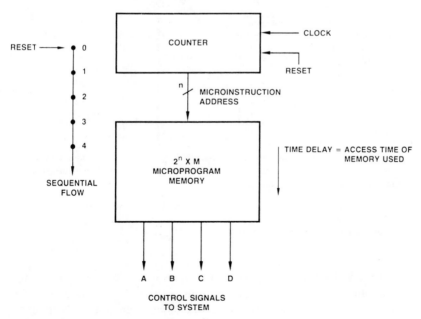

Figure 2-2.   Sequential control.

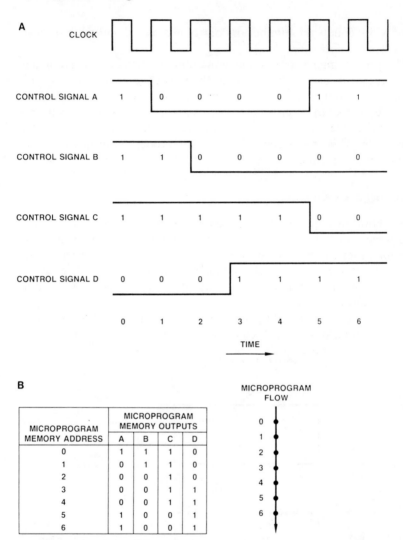

Figure 2–3. Sample sequential microcode. (A) Desired control. Assume that this is the desired control for some system. (B) Microcode and flow. This is then the microcode for sequential execution.

which is approximately the same as before, since

$$t_{\text{read access}} \gg t_{C_p \text{ to output}}$$

To derive the control portion of the microcode for either of the two control units described so far, assume a timing diagram exists. By digitizing the timing signals using the clock step and assuming all changes correspond to the rising edge of the clock, the microprogram

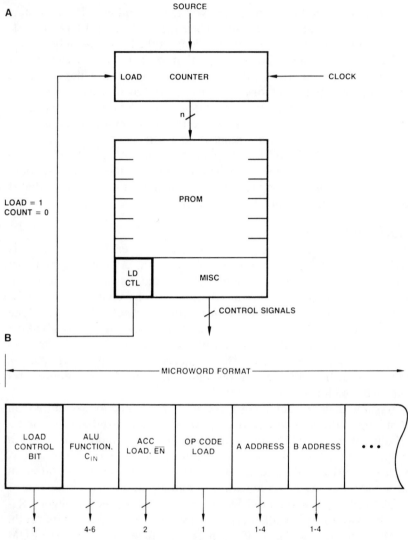

Figure 2–4. Multiple sequence controller. (A) Controller. (B) Microword format.
(Load cont., load control)

control field is simply the binary word at each time slice. The procedure is shown in Figure 2-3.

Multiple Sequences

The controller may be made to execute several sequences by adding one control bit to the word width, the load control bit. This bit connects to the load control line of the loadable counter, as shown in Figure 2-4.

The data inputs to the counter receive the start address. The new start address is gated into the counter when the load control bit equals 1. The counter operates as a counter as long as the load control bit equals 0. Each microroutine or microinstruction sequence would contain a 1 in the load control field in the last microinstruction of the sequence only and a 0 in that field for all other microinstructions.

The size of the PROM memory is determined by the total number of microinstructions it must store. Since PROM memories come only in certain sizes, a "ballpark" number is sufficient for selection. The smallest sizes are 32 by 8 (nonregistered) and 512 by 18 (registered PROM). The number of address bits required and the size of the counter are determined by the amount of the memory that is used or that is anticipated to be used in later enhancements.

Start Addresses

If the controller is a CCU, the start address of each microroutine is derived from the current machine instruction. At the minimum, an instruction register must be added between the data bus and the counter data inputs to store this instruction. A load control bit must be added to the microword for the instruction register, which must load prior to the counter load (see Figure 2-5). This scheme requires that the op code equal the high-order bits of the start address, with the low-order bits tied to logical 0. This is necessary to allow the starting addresses to be separated by the minimum number of addresses required by the longest microroutine.

Assume that no machine instruction is anticipated to take more than 16 microinstructions to execute. Also, assume a 12-bit address and a 4K PROM memory. The op code must then be no more than 8 bits in length, and the lower 4 bits of the counter data inputs must be tied low. Sixteen steps are allowed per microroutine, and up to 256 different start addresses are possible with this configuration.

The clock pulse required by the controller has not changed. Remember also that the width of the memory is not a function of its depth.

This scheme is adequate if (1) there is sufficient room in the PROM memory, (2) spare locations are acceptable, and (3) no microroutine exceeds 16 steps. If a microroutine exceeds 16 steps, it would overrun a start address, reducing the number of op codes possible; this may still be acceptable. Short routines leave discontinuous unused areas scattered throughout the PROM memory; this may also be acceptable.

Mapping PROM

If fragmented space and reduced available op codes are not acceptable, one solution is to add a mapping PROM between the instruction register and the counter. The op code is the address into the map, which in

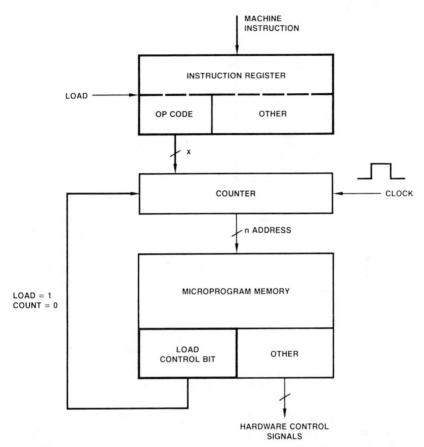

Figure 2–5.   Basic CCU. (x, number of bits in op code; n, number of bits in counter address)

turn outputs the full start address of the microroutine to the counter, as shown in Figure 2-6. Start addresses may now be assigned at any location in the PROM memory rather than being equidistant from one another, and routines may be compacted to delete excessive frag- mented space. (It is a good idea to allow some unused areas within the PROM to allow for enhancement changes.) The final placement of the routines in the production PROMs should be done after the debug cycle to minimize mapping PROM changes. This is where a development system is used to advantage.

   Another feature may be added once a mapping PROM approach is chosen. The mapping PROM may be made larger than required for normal running and contain address lines driven by switches to allow a

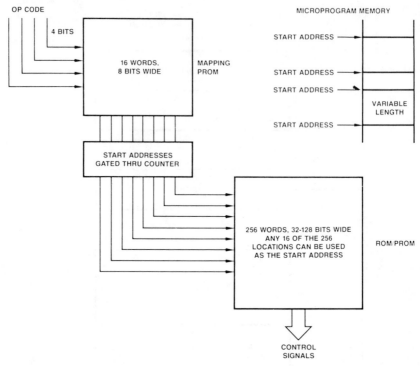

Figure 2–6. Mapping PROM.

Privileged State, where all op codes are valid, and a Normal State, where certain op codes are invalid, "trapping out" to an error trap address in the control memory. The control memory would not necessarily be larger than before.

Also, the mapping PROM and the PROM memory may be set up for future expansion and expansion address lines merely left disconnected or the PROMs left unused in the added areas. (The usual approach is to leave the PROM chips off the board.) It is easier to provide for expansion now than to do a redesign later.

The CCU is shown in Figure 2-7. A fairly reasonable control system has been constructed which is acceptable if all of the microroutines are simple sequences.

Unconditional Branch

Often routines may start differently but end with the same steps. Also, once starting addresses are mapped, it might be found that a routine needs to be extended. For these and other cases, the existence of a GO TO or unconditional branch next-address control is desirable. The in-

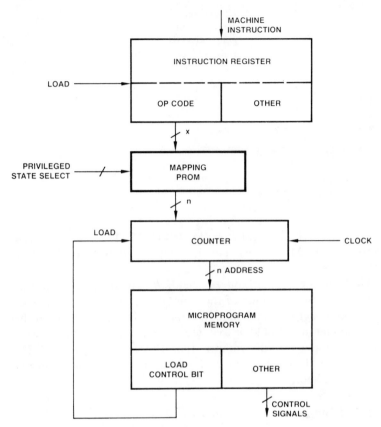

Figure 2-7. CCU with mapping PROM.

struction flow is shown in Figure 2-8. This instruction causes the counter to be loaded with the desired next address, which is not in sequence
with the current address. This is not a start address; therefore the map
is not involved. Instead, the microword width must be expanded as
shown in Figure 2-9 to contain a branch address field, up to n bits wide,
and a next-address-select field. The map and the branch address lines
would be input to a 1-of-2 MUX network, n bits wide, with the MUX
select operated by the address selection field of the microword. The
MUX outputs are the inputs to the counter, as shown in Figure 2-10.

A sample piece of microcode, shown in Figure 2-11, highlights the
load control to the counter, the address MUX select, and the branch
address field. Assume that the program start address is at address 50.
Execution is then seen to be sequential until address 53, which loads
the counter (LDCTL = 1) with a branch address (ADR MUX = 0)
supplied at address 53 (BR ADR = 90). The next microinstruction executed is at address 90. Address 90 causes a branch back to address 13.

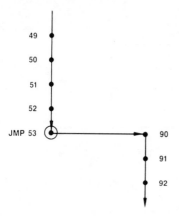

Figure 2–8. Flow diagram of unconditional jump—the GO TO statement. (JMP, jump)

Address 14 causes the counter to be loaded (LDCTL = 1) with a new start address (ADR MUX = 1). This is the last step in the routine that began at address 50.

The width of the branch address field, B, could be less than n, restricting the allowable range of the branch (for example, by leaving the $n - B$ high-order bits unchanged). This complicates the task for the microprogrammer and should be avoided by beginning designers. Good programming practices will require that the various parts of the routines be kept in a relatively compact area, if possible, *without* artificial enforcement.

Conditional Branch

It is sometimes desirable to terminate a microroutine in one of several different ways depending on one or more conditions. The conditions tested could be the various status bit outputs of the ALU based on the result of an operation, such as (1) $Z = 1$ if ACC = 0, (2) $S = 1$ if

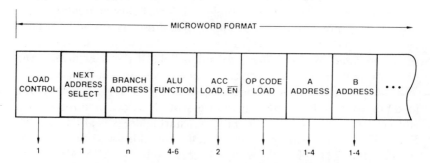

Figure 2–9. Expanded microword. Width of microword increases with increased flexibility and control.

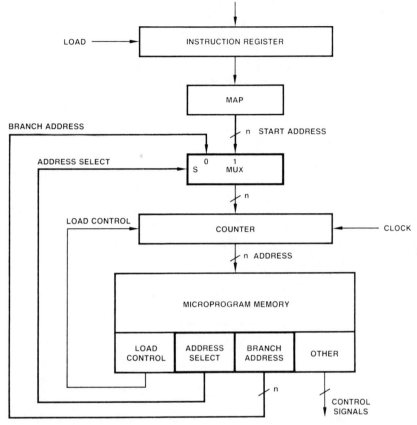

Figure 2–10.   CCU with branch capability.

ACC < 0, (3) C_{out} = 1 if $|ACC|$ > range, (4) OVR (overflow) = 1 if error, or (5) on the result of a compare operation. Only one condition is testable at a time. Hardware could be used to combine a number of conditions and to supply one test bit if that combination is expected to occur frequently. A program slow diagram for a conditional branch is shown in Figure 2-12.

The ability to test a condition and to branch if the condition is true is provided by adding a MUX at the counter load control. The load control field in the microword is changed to a branch condition select, which selects (1) ground (count; no branch), (2) condition 1 or condition 2 (load branch address into counter if true), or (3) Vcc (unconditional branch, load counter). The CCU is shown in Figure 2-13, with its microword format shown in Figure 12-14.

A sample piece of microcode is shown in Figure 2-15 that has both unconditional and conditional branches. As with most programming

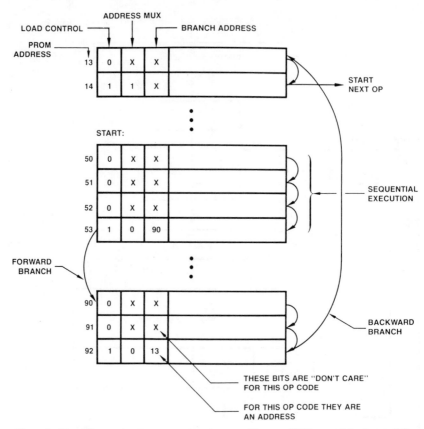

Figure 2–11. Microcode, demonstrating the use of jumps. (X bits are "don't care" for this op code; numbered bits are addresses for this op code.)

languages, if a conditional test fails, execution continues sequentially, as shown in statements at addresses 30 and 31. The branch condition select field is 2 bits wide in this example. A wider field would allow a larger MUX and therefore would allow more conditions to be tested.

Timing Considerations

The basic controller evolved so far can be a primitive CCU. Figure 2-16 shows the connections between this CCU and the ALU portions of the simple system described earlier.

The clock pulse width, called the microcycle, is determined from

$$\underline{C}_p = \overline{t}_{\text{counter clock to output}} + \overline{t}_{\text{PROM read access}} + \overline{t}_{\text{ALU execution}}$$

(For the 2900 family a microcycle is measured from one rising edge

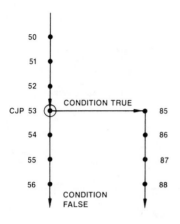

Figure 2–12. Conditional branch flow diagram. "IF-THEN-ELSE" — the conditional branch. (CJP, conditional jump)

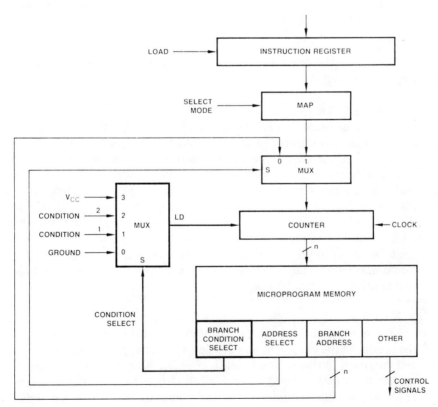

Figure 2–13. CCU with conditional branch capability.

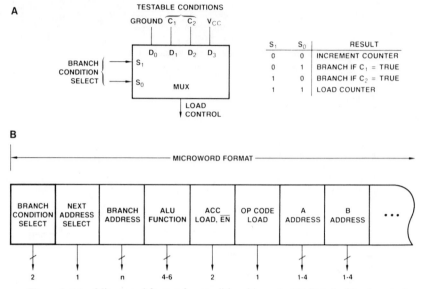

Figure 2–14. Microword format for conditional branch. (A) Detail of load control MUX. (B) Detail of microword format.

of the clock to the next. All register write operations occur on the rising edge of the clock.)

Sequential Timing

A timing diagram is given in Figure 2-17 showing a series of sequential program steps (refer to the CCU-ALU of Figure 2-16). At each rising edge of the clock, the counter increments and settles, and the counter outputs an address to the PROM, whose access time is greater than the counter settling time. As soon as the outputs are stable at the PROM output, execution begins in the ALU. (For now, assume that the operands are available.) On the next rising edge of the clock, the ALU result is gated into the accumulator and the status signals which are being input to the condition MUX are assumed to be stable. (They would normally be gated into a status register on the same clock edge that loads the accumulator.)

Branching

Now assume that a conditional branch is to be executed. On the rising edge of the clock, the status signals from the previous instruction and the result of that instruction are available. Concurrently, the counter has been incremented (Figure 2-18). (Note: this counter is a synchronous loading counter.) The microinstruction $i + 1$ has been fetched, and this is the conditional branch.

When the outputs are available from the PROM memory, the control signals are sent to the counter to cause it to load the branch address *if* the tested condition is true. The MUX select bits, and the condition inputs propagate through the MUX prior to the next rising edge of the clock. No ALU activity occurs.

On the next rising edge of the clock, the branch address enters the counter and the address is input to the PROM. Execution proceeds as before.

There is no difference in the instruction cycle of a branch and a nonbranch instruction in this system. However, while the memory is being accessed, the ALU must remain idle, and while the ALU executes, the memory must remain idle. The minimum total width of the microcycle, C_μ, is the sum of the worst case fetch and execute times.

Pipelining

To improve speed, it is desirable to allow overlap of the ALU and memory fetch processes. This is possible by adding a register at the PROM output, called a pipeline register. The counter is acting as

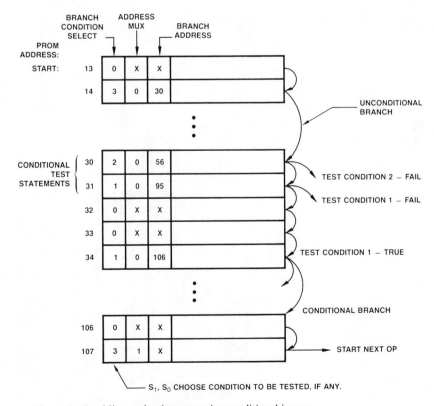

Figure 2–15. Microcode, demonstrating conditional jumps.

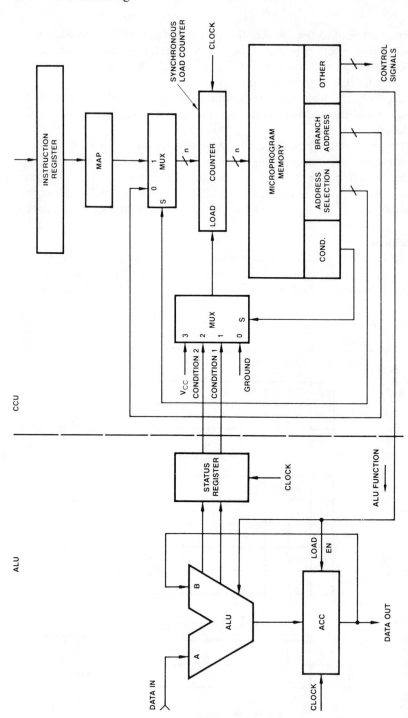

Figure 2-16.   Elementary system.

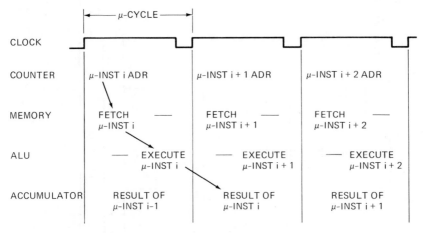

Figure 2–17. Microcycle timing for the system of Figure 2–16 (no branch).

another pipeline register, holding the address that the memory is fetching. The PROM pipeline will hold the current microinstruction under execution. This will allow the counter to move one count ahead and therefore will allow a memory fetch of the $i + 1$st microinstruction to be overlapped with the execution of the ith microinstruction. The configuration is shown in Figure 2-19.

Figure 2-20 shows the timing diagram for sequential execution of this system. When the counter contains the address of microinstruction i, the memory is fetching microinstruction i. The pipeline register con-

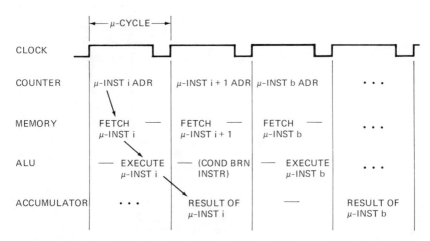

Figure 2–18. Microcycle timing for the system of Figure 2–16 (branch). Conditional branch on result of previous microinstruction.

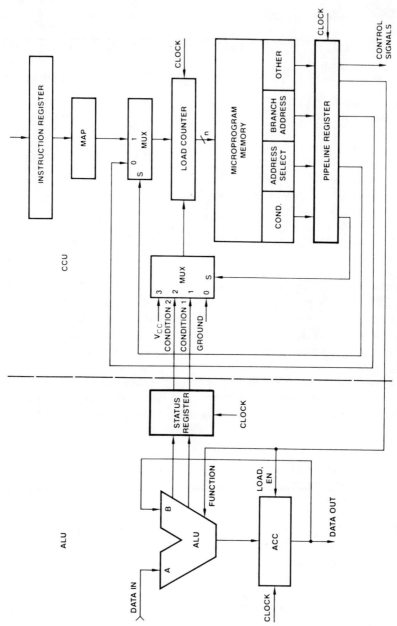

Figure 2–19. Simple system with a pipeline register added. (Reg., register.)

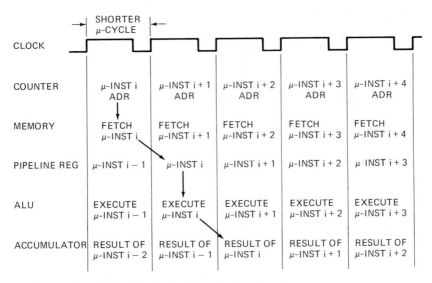

Figure 2–20.   Timing for the pipeline system, no branch.

tains microinstruction $i - 1$, which is under execution. If the microinstruction uses the ALU, the ALU is executing the commands of microinstruction $i - 1$ at this time. The accumulator contains the result of the execution of microinstruction $i - 2$; hence the reference to a two-level pipeline.

On the rising edge of the next clock, the counter increments and the memory proceeds to fetch microinstruction $i + 1$. The pipeline loads with the outputs of the previous memory fetch, microinstruction i, and execution proceeds as before.

The microcycle (no branch) is now

$$\underline{C}_p = \bar{t}_{\text{counter clock to output}} + \bar{t}_{\text{PROM read access}}$$

or

$$\underline{C}_p = \bar{t}_{\text{pipeline clock to output}} + \bar{t}_{\text{ALU execution}}$$

whichever is greater. If we reasonably assume that the PROM read access time is not longer than the ALU execute time, then the second equation dominates.

Pipeline Branch

Figure 2-21 examines what happens in this case when a branch is executed. On the rising edge of the first clock, the address of microinstruction i is in the counter and memory is fetching the microinstruction at this address. Execution proceeds as before until the third clock

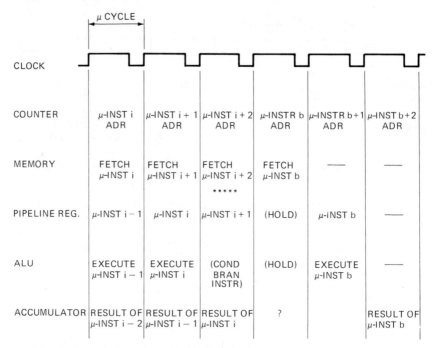

Figure 2-21.   Timing for the pipeline system, branch on result.

signal. At this point the address of microinstruction $i + 2$ is in the counter and the memory is fetching microinstruction $i + 2$.

Microinstruction $i + 1$ is in the pipeline register; this is the conditional branch instruction. The result of microinstruction i is in the accumulator, and the status bits for the ALU produced by the execution of microinstruction i are available. The conditional branch causes the control signals to select the condition to be tested and sets up the load-counter-if-true conditions.

On the next clock edge, microinstruction $i + 2$ *cannot be loaded* into the pipeline. A control signal must block one clock pulse to the pipeline register. The branch address is loaded into the counter, and the memory fetches this address. The pipeline still contains microinstruction $i + 1$, the branch instruction which must not reexecute. Essentially, the execute phase is rendered idle during this microcycle. The next rising edge of the clock loads the branched-to address into the pipeline, and execution proceeds as before.

The problems are obvious. First, a control field and possibly some SSI/MSI controls must be added to prevent cyclic execution of the conditional branch instruction. Second, for one microcycle the ALU is idle and for two microcycles the ACC is unchanged. The process is referred to as "flushing" the pipeline on execution of a branch instruction; since we have a two-level pipeline, it takes two microcycles to refill the pipe or to recover. This is not desirable if we branch often in a program because the time gained by overlapping memory fetch and ALU execution will be lost. We will ignore the extra hardware and implied programming constraints.

Improved Architecture

The CCU is improved by placing the next-address MUX to input directly into the PROM to avoid the counter setup time. The counter then becomes one of the three inputs into the next-address MUX. The condition select MUX must be replaced by equivalent logic to generate the two MUX select signals of the new next address MUX.

The counter has moved to a position where it cannot receive a proper input. It must be replaced with a register, called the microprogram counter (μPC) which is connected to the next-address MUX input, formerly assigned to the counter. An incrementer is connected to the PROM memory input and outputs to the μPC. The incrementer always contains the address being fetched plus 1. The outputs of the incrementer are gated into the μPC on the rising edge of the clock. The resulting configuration is shown in Figure 2-22.

No Branch

The timing diagram for Figure 2-22 for no-branch execution is shown in Figure 2-23. What exists now is a three-level pipeline. During the first microcycle, the memory is fetching microinstruction i. The address of microinstruction i is in the μPC. The incrementer is one instruction ahead, with the address of microinstruction $i + 1$. The pipeline register contains microinstruction $i - 1$, which is in execution. The accumulator contains the results of microinstruction $i - 2$. The execution proceeds as in earlier diagrams.

Improved Branching

The difference between the designs is shown in the activity which occurs when a branch is executed, as shown in Figure 2-24.

On the second clock, the memory is fetching microinstruction $i + 1$, and the address of microinstruction $i + 1$ is in the μPC. The address of microinstruction $i + 2$ is in the incrementer. Microinstruction i is in the pipeline register and is being executed by the ALU. The result of microinstruction $i - 1$ is in the accumulator.

On the next clock, microinstruction $i + 1$ is loaded into the pipeline register. This is the conditional branch. The pipeline outputs the controls to the condition select logic which switches the MUX to pass the branch address. At the instant that the clock edge comes up, the μPC is

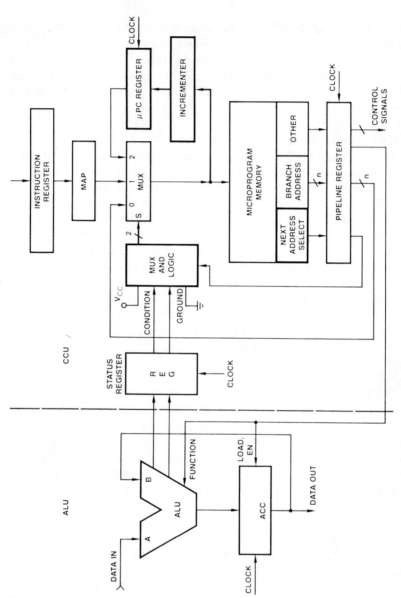

Figure 2–22.   Completed elementary system.

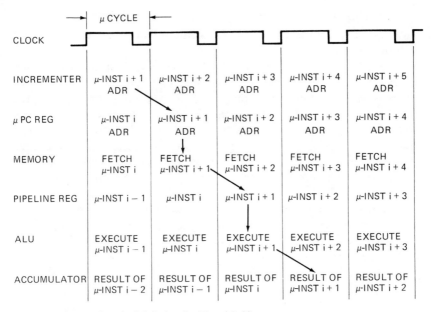

Figure 2–23.   Sequential timing for Figure 2–22.

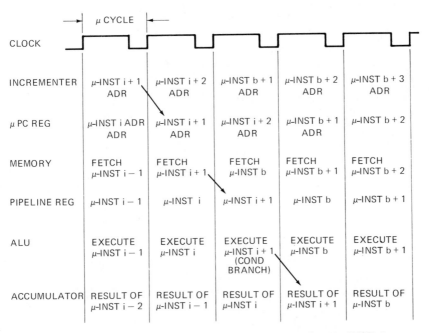

Figure 2–24.   Timing to "branch on result" of (microinstruction i (μ-INST. i).

loaded with the address of microinstruction $i + 2$. As soon as the outputs are available, if the MUX has not yet switched, address $i + 2$ will be sent to memory.

The read access time of the PROM is greater than the propagation delay of the path through the pipeline, condition MUX, and next-address MUX and is greater than the μPC register setup time and the propagation delay of its output through the next-address MUX. Any fluttering of the address inputs occurring from the start of a fetch of microinstruction $i + 2$ and then the switch to the fetch of the branch address is irrelevant, since the memory output is not sensed until the next clock. Therefore during the third cycle the branch address is fetched.

The incrementer now contains the address following the branch address. On the next clock, execution proceeds with no flushing of the pipe, with no extraordinary idle times. This is the desired CCU design.

The cycle time is now

$$\underline{C}_p = \bar{t}_{\substack{\text{pipeline clock} \\ \text{to output}}} \quad + \bar{t}_{\substack{\text{propagate} \\ \text{cond. logic}}} \quad + \bar{t}_{\substack{\text{propagate} \\ \text{next-address MUX}}}$$

$$+ \bar{t}_{\substack{\text{PROM read} \\ \text{access}}} \quad + \bar{t}_{\substack{\text{register setup} \\ \text{(pipeline)}}}$$

or

$$\underline{C}_p = \bar{t}_{\text{setup } \mu\text{PC}} \quad + \bar{t}_{\substack{\text{propagate} \\ \text{next-address MUX}}} \quad + \bar{t}_{\substack{\text{PROM read} \\ \text{access}}} \quad + \bar{t}_{\substack{\text{register setup} \\ \text{(pipeline)}}}$$

or

$$\underline{C}_p = \bar{t}_{\substack{\text{pipeline clock} \\ \text{to output}}} \quad + \bar{t}_{\text{ALU execution}} \quad + \bar{t}_{\substack{\text{register setup} \\ \text{(ACC; status)}}}$$

whichever is *longer* (whichever is the *critical path*).

3

Adding Programming Support to the Controller

The CCU developed in Chapter 2 is a high-speed unit capable of making decisions and branching around in the PROM control memory. Any problem may be programmed if GO TO and IF equivalent programming structures exist. The limitations are (1) available programming time, (2) available programming skill, and (3) allowable memory size. The resulting program will run but will be messy at best. As the complexity of the application increases, the need for more powerful programming capabilities increases.

Expanded Testing

The first change is to expand the number of testable conditions. This is easily done by expanding the branch condition selection MUX which inputs to the next-address MUX selection logic. Next, allow testing to be for IF C_i or for IF NOT C_i. This is done by adding a polarity select bit to the microword and a polarity logic block between the condition MUX and the next-address logic block. This improved CCU is shown in Figure 3-1.

Subroutines

Up to this point, when a branch is executed, the only way to return from the branched-to routine is to execute another branch, and the programmer has to know the exact address. This is fine as long as the

43

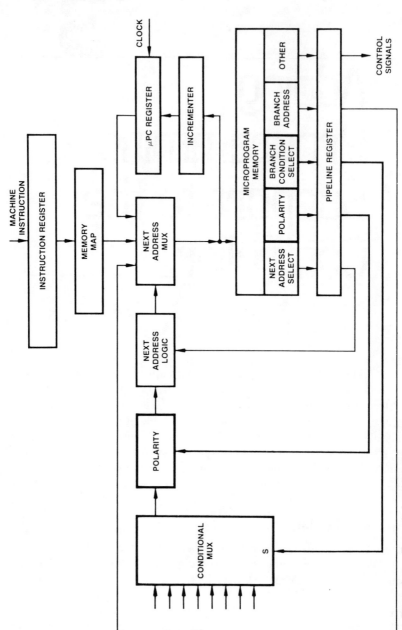

Figure 3–1. Expanded conditional testing.

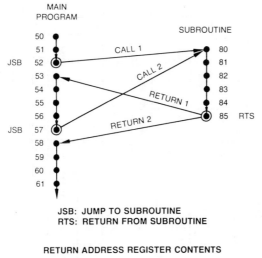

MAIN PROGRAM

SUBROUTINE

JSB: JUMP TO SUBROUTINE
RTS: RETURN FROM SUBROUTINE

RETURN ADDRESS REGISTER CONTENTS

START	AFTER 52	AFTER 85	AFTER 57
λ	53	λ	58

Figure 3–2.   Subroutine flow. (JSB, jump to subroutine; RTS, return from subroutine; λ, garbage.)

branched-to code is accessed by only one source and is required to return to only one source or calling location. When two or more micro-routines need to branch to the same piece of code and it is necessary to return from executing that code to the individual calling routine, GO TO and IF structures are inadequate.

It is desirable to provide, instead, a means of storing the address of the calling statement and a means of accessing this storage for the return address. This ability in a higher-level programming language exists as subroutines or procedures.

A subroutine can be called from anywhere in a program, and the return to the next statement following the calling statement is made either upon completion of the execution of the subroutine—an uncon-ditional return—or upon the successful test of a condition—a condi-tional return. Subroutines should be more than one or two statements long to avoid choppy code. (Debug and maintenance features must be stressed in any large microprogram, just as they are in any other pro-gramming language.)

A flow of a subroutine calling program is shown in Figure 3-2. When the statement at address 52 calls the subroutine, address 53 is pushed into the return address store. When the return statement at address 85

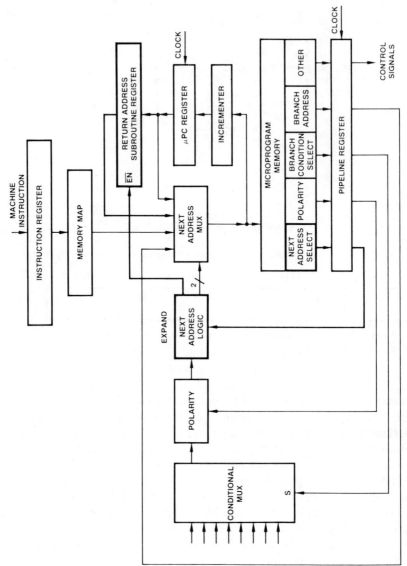

Figure 3–3. CCU with subroutine ability.

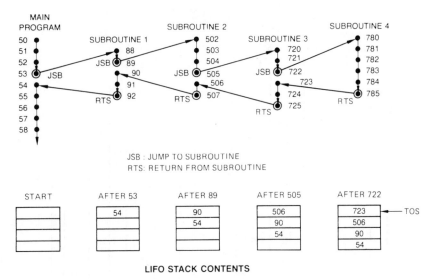

JSB : JUMP TO SUBROUTINE
RTS: RETURN FROM SUBROUTINE

LIFO STACK CONTENTS

Figure 3–4.   Nested subroutine flow.

is executed, the return address is popped from the store which provides the address of the next microinstruction.

The hardware required to enable the CCU to do this is shown in Figure 3-3. The next-address select logic is expanded to add a load enable to the return address register. When a CALL instruction is executed, a branch to the subroutine is handled as any other branch with the addition that the contents of the μPC are copied into the return address register. The incrementer contains the address of the second step of the subroutine.

To return, the RETURN statement will cause the next-address MUX to select the return address register outputs as the source of the next PROM address, with execution proceeding as if an unconditional branch had occurred.

Nested Subroutines

Nested subroutines are flow diagrammed in Figure 3-4. Nested subroutines require more than one return address location and a means of keeping track of the order of the calls. This is accomplished by using a LIFO (last in, first out) stack, *pushing* and address onto the stack when a CALL is executed and *popping* an address off, when a RETURN is executed. A stack pointer is used to point to the last entry, which is the top of the stack (TOS).

The same rules that exist for any programming language apply for nested subroutines. When subroutines are nested, the call returns are

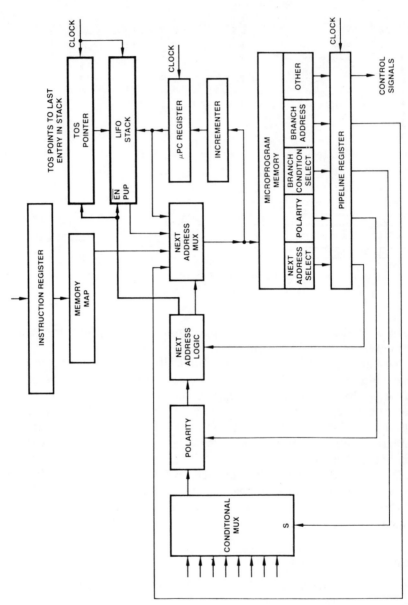

Figure 3–5. Adding the FILO stack and TOS pointer.

treated as parentheses in an algebraic equation—that is, if subroutine 3 calls subroutine 4, then subroutine 4 returns to a point in subroutine 3. Subroutine 4 cannot jump out of the subroutine nest in one step. Each return address must be popped from the stack in the order in which it was pushed onto the stack. The TOS pointer can be incremented (for a PUSH) or decremented (for a POP) only by 1.

The hardware to allow this is shown in Figure 3-5. A LIFO stack replaces the return address register, and a TOS pointer, a simple counter, has been added. The next-address logic is expanded to provide load enable and PUSH/POP controls to the stack and increment/decrement (INC/DEC) controls to the pointer.

When a subroutine is called, the branch address passes as before. The TOS pointer is incremented, and the μPC is moved into the LIFO stack to the position indexed by the TOS pointer. When a return statement is executed, the contents of the stack location referenced by the TOS pointer are gated by the next-address select MUX into the PROM memory. On the next cycle the TOS pointer is decremented.

Stack Size

How large a stack is necessary? Since this stack is to handle microprogram subroutines and since the microprogram is composed of a number of microroutines which also modularize it, deep subroutine nesting is not desirable, nor is it necessary in the general case. For this CCU, a stack four deep is provided and assumed to be adequate. Depending on the ability of the stack to wrap, that is, if the pointer can move from position 4, binary address 11, to position 1, binary address 00 on the fifth successive PUSH without any intervening POP, various types of disasters can occur. The stack may or may not signal that it is full, depending on implementation details. The programmer is cautioned.

Loops

Another desirable programming feature is the ability to repeat one or more statements for some number of times until the number of specified repeats has been completed or until some specified condition occurs. To handle such loops, the starting address must be storable and retrievable and a decrementing or incrementing counter must be provided. The CCU under construction will use a decrementing settable counter. A basic program flow for a loop is shown in Figure 3-6.

Tristate Lines

The hardware required will require a few changes in the basic CCU. First, there are no more available inputs into the next-address MUX. Rather than expand from a 1-of-4 to a 1-of-8 MUX, which would in-

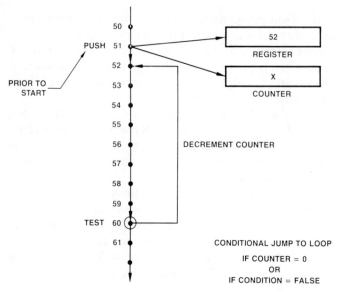

Figure 3–6.   Loop flow. Conditional jump-to loop (CJP) activated if counter ≠ 0, or if CONDITION = FALSE.

crease the microword size, we choose instead to reroute the pipeline branch address lines and have the branch address lines share one of the MUX inputs with the mapping PROM, since a start address and a branch address will never occur at the same time. To allow this sharing, the branch address portion of the pipeline register and the mapping PROM outputs must be tristate lines and must have output enable control signals supplied by the next-address select logic.

Start Address Storage
The register used to store the start address of the loop is added in parallel with the address bus and may be loaded from the mapping PROM or from the pipeline branch address field. The register is connected to the next-address MUX. Register loading must be controlled by either the next-address logic control or by microinstruction control.

Counter
A counter is added such that it is loadable from the mapping PROM or the pipeline branch address field. The technique of allowing a microword format field to be an address in one instruction and a count value in another instruction is called overlapping. The next-address control logic must control the load enable and the decrement control of the counter. The counter provides a status input to the condition MUX, which is used to determine when the contents of the decrementing counter reaches 0. The hardware is shown in Figure 3-7.

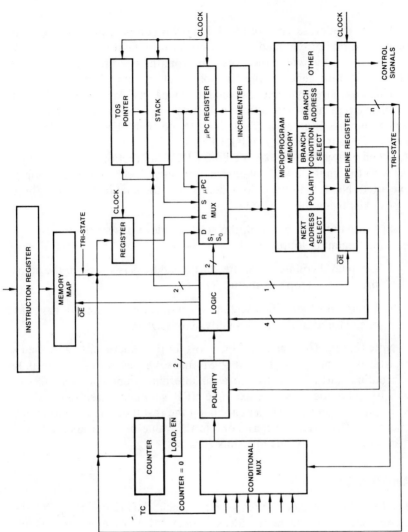

Figure 3–7. CCU with loop ability.

Am29811

The next-address control block is now a complex piece of logic. It receives 4 bits of encoded instruction from its field in the microword format $(I_0 - I_3)$ and also receives 1 bit from the condition MUX output (TEST). It must generate the control signals given in Table 3-1.

This logic already exists as a single device, the Am29811. The 4 bits of instruction allow 16 different instructions to be generated; their mnemonic list is given in Table 3-2. (Note that TEST is active high, i.e., a test fails if TEST $\neq$ HIGH.)

When a loop is to be executed, an LDCT instruction loads the counter with the limit value. This instruction must occur before the loop is executed. Next, the type of loop determines the loop instruction. Three types exist using the Am29811:

1. Loop until counter $\neq 0$, the starting address is stored in last statement of loop; RPCT.

2. Loop until counter $= 0$, the starting address is stored in the stack prior to the loop beginning; RFCT.

3. Loop until a specified test is successful; the starting address has been stored in the stack in advance; LOOP.

Note that the CCU as developed was for the general case and used a register with the loops. The Am29811 uses the register as an alternate subroutine start address (R_i) or as an alternate branch address in two-way jump instructions. For example, JRP is a jump to register address R_i or pipeline address D_i depending on the result of a test. During any microcycle, the register may contain the value of the branch address from any of the previous microinstructions.

Am2909/11

The CCU logic blocks, the register, the stack, the pointer, the μPC, the incrementer, and the next-address select MUX all exist as a single device, the Am2909/11 microprogram sequencer (see Figure 3-8).

Table 3–1   Am29811 Control Signals

Signal	Definition
$\overline{\text{MAP E}}$	Output enable, mapping PROM
$\overline{\text{PLE}}$	Output enable, pipeline
S_1, S_0	2 bits of next-address MUX select
$\overline{\text{FE}}$	File (stack) enable
PUP	Stack PUSH/POP control
$\overline{\text{CNT LOAD}}$	Counter load enable
$\overline{\text{CNT E}}$	Counter decrement enable

Table 3–2   Am29811 Instruction Table

CJP	Conditional jump pipeline (jump if)
CJPP	Conditional jump pipeline: POP stack
CJS	Conditional jump subroutine from pipeline (and PUSH)
CJV	Conditional jump vector (interrupt)
CONT	Continue (μpc$\leftarrow\mu$pc$+1$)
CRTN	Conditional return (and POP)
JMAP	Jump to map address (next op)
JP	Jump to pipeline address (branch)
JRP	Conditional jump register or pipeline
JSRP	Conditional jump subroutine from register or pipeline (and PUSH)
JZ	Jump to address zero (initialize)
LDCT	Load counter and continue
LOOP	Repeat loop, TEST = FAIL, from stack
PUSH	Push stack: conditional load counter and continue
RFCT	Repeat loop, counter $\neq$ 0, from stack
RPCT	Repeat loop, counter $\neq$ 0, from pipeline

The Am2909 and Am2911 differ in package size. The Am2911 has one input to the D (direct) position of the next-address MUX, which is shared with the input to the register (R), while the Am2909 has separate inputs for each. The Am2909 also has OR inputs which allow the outputs of the CCU to be ORed logically with outside data.

Both the Am2909 and Am2911 are bit-slice devices, 4 bits wide and expandable to any width. The typical configuration is three Am2909/11 units and one Am29811. The devices are tied together through the C_{in} and C_{out} lines of the incrementer.

Three devices can access 2^{12} words or a 4K ROM memory. A reasonably sized CCU might have a PROM memory between 4K and 16K. Controllers have smaller memories, usually less than 4K, depending on the particular application.

CASE Statement (Am29803)

There is one other desirable programming structure, the CASE statement or n-way branch. With conditional testing via IF structures, one test is made at a time and branching is to one of two locations. An n-way branch performs one test and branches to one of n locations.

The Am29803 is a testing matrix which connects to the OR inputs of the Am2909. Up to four test inputs may be connected to the Am29803 inputs. A 4-bit encoded instruction selects none, one, two, three, or all four test inputs to produce up to a 16-way branch in one step.

As a sample application consider the situation where two Am2911 units supply the eight high-order address bits and an Am2909 supplies the last four bits. When a test is to be done, the branch address of the

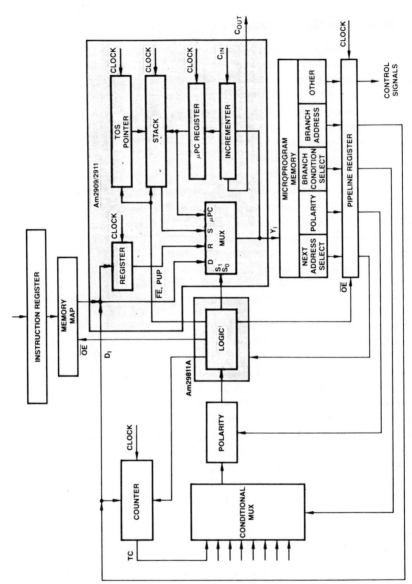

Figure 3–8.   CCU with Am2909, Am29811A.

start of the branch table is output by the sequencers. With the configuration indicated, the branch table *must* be located within the microprogram memory so that its first address ends in four zeros (binary). The test produces four bits which are internally ORed to the Am2909 outputs and which select the specific address within the branch table. The branch table is nothing more than a set of jump instructions.

Suppose that you are to test four conditions and decide what to do next, based on the results of the four tests. The software would contain 15 jump instructions for testing, and it would be necessary to execute four instructions to complete the decision. With the Am29803, the four tests are input and an encoded result produced. A 15-deep jump instruction branch table is sufficient, and only two jump instructions need to be executed, one to the branch table and one as a result of landing within the table.

To use the Am29803, a four-bit instruction field must be added to the microword. A branch instruction is executed with the pipeline field supplying the Am29803 instruction to be executed in parallel with the Am2909 instruction. Since the branch address is the one produced by ORing the Am29803 outputs to the Am2909, the Am29803 is disabled by sending the appropriate instruction and execution continues. A typical CCU structure with some Am2909/11 units, an Am29811A, and an Am29803 is given in Figure 3-9.

Microprogram Memory

The microprogram memory is implemented in ROMs when a final design is debugged and a high volume production run is anticipated. ROMs carry a mask charge for their factory programming, and the production volume must be sufficient to absorb this charge. Low volume production and prototypes are implemented in PROMs, erasable PROMs (EPROMs), or writable control stores. In the PROM family, registered PROMs, memories with on-board pipeline registers, also exist.

Am27S27

The Am27S27 is a registered PROM. It is organized as a 512 by 8 array, with nine address lines and two enable lines. The worst-case time between the address being presented and the data being ready to enter the register is 50 ns and referred to as the address to C_p (high) set-up time, t_s (A). The register must be output enabled, $\overline{E_1}$ and $\overline{E_2}$ both low, and clocked to load the data. Data are available at the output in 20 ns worst case, referred to as the delay from C_p (high) to output t_{PHL} (C_p), t_{PLH} (C_p), assuming that the chip is already enabled. (Refer to the Am27S27 data sheet.) If not, the time delay is 25 ns worst case.

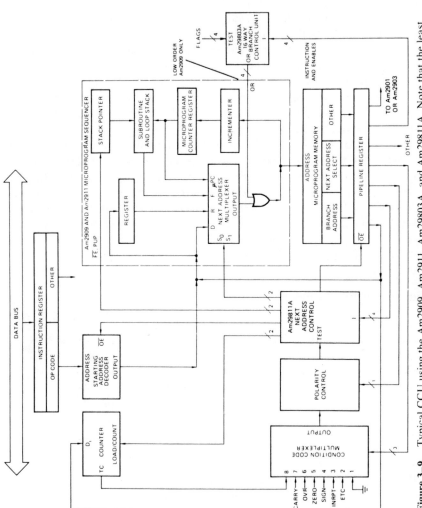

Figure 3–9. Typical CCU using the Am2909, Am2911, Am2903A, and Am29811A. Note that the least significant microprogram sequencer is an Am2909 and the more significant sequencers are Am2911 units.

Only that portion of the microword containing the branch address need be under output enable control. The remaining output enables may be used to allow large PROM memories to be constructed. Most microwords are 32–96 bits in length; most microprogram memories are 1K–4K words deep.

Sample Design

Assume that a 512 by 80 memory is desired. Using the Am27S27 (tristate), ten chips must be placed in parallel with all address and enable lines common (Figure 3-10).

The first item that needs to be investigated is dc loading. Assume that the memory is connected to three Am2911 microprogram sequencers, which provide the required 9-bit address ($2^9 = 512$). Each address line carries ten times the loading represented by one Am27S27.

From the data sheets, we get the information in Table 3-3.

The Am2911 can drive

$$\frac{I_{OL} \text{ of Am2911}}{I_{IL} \text{ of Am27S27}} = \frac{12.0}{0.25} = 48$$

loads. The 512 × 80 memory presents ten loads; thus there is no problem here.

What about the ac loading? The Am27S27 will present a capacitive load of 10 × 5 pf = 50 pf, which, in the Am2911 specification, is the number for which the Am2911 timing is characterized; therefore there will be no degradation of Am2911 performance.

Sample Design 2

Assume that a 2K × 80 memory is desired.

This requires that an Am25LS139 decoder (or comparable device) be used to decode the two added high-order address bits into output enable $\overline{E}_2$ signals. Three Am2911 units are required to supply the 11-bit address. The configuration is shown in Figure 3-11, which details the basic interconnections. The address lines are loaded with 4 × 10 = 40 loads, under the 48 load limit; therefore no buffer drivers are required.

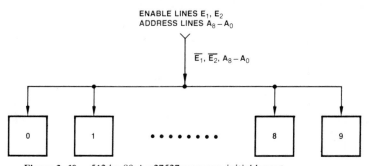

ENABLE LINES E_1, E_2
ADDRESS LINES $A_8 - A_0$

$\overline{E}_1$, $\overline{E}_2$, $A_8 - A_0$

| 0 | 1 | • • • • • • • • | 8 | 9 |

Figure 3–10.   512 by 80 Am27527 memory, initial layout.

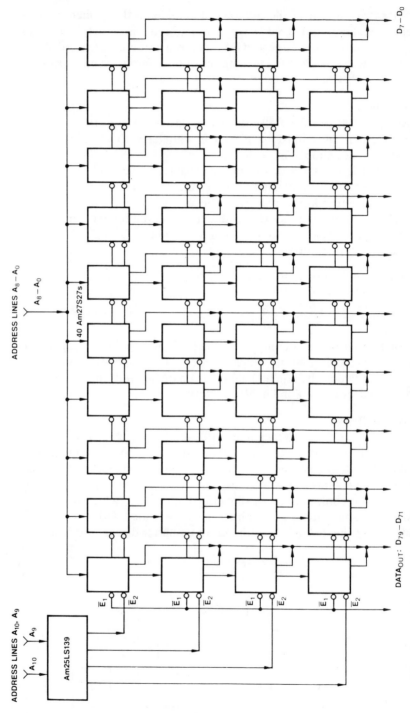

Figure 3–11.   2K by 80 Am27527 memory. Only one "row" of 27527s are enabled at any one time.

Table 3-3   Data on dc Loading

Parameter	Am2911	Am27S27	Low Power Schottky
V_{OH}	2.4 V		
I_{OH}	-2.6 mA		
V_{OL}	0.5 V		
I_{OL}	12 mA		
V_{IH}		2.0 V	2.0 V
I_{IH}		25 A	20 A
V_{IL}		0.8 V	0.8 V
I_{IL}		-0.25 mA	-0.4 mA
C_{in}		5 pf	

The Am27S27S are switched by row and are not always enabled. When the enable signal is switched, there is an added delay of 5 ns using t_{PZL} (C_p), t_{PZH} (C_p) as the device switches from its high-impedance state to active output, making the total delay from clock to output 25 ns worst case.

The ac loading is significant with 40×5 pf = 200 pf loading on each Am2911 address line.

The Am2911 performance must be degraded in accordance with this increased capacitive load by 0.1 ns per pf over 50 pf:

200 pf $-$ 50 pf $=$ 150 pf

0.1 ns/pf $\times$ 150 pf $=$ 15 ns added delay to the Am2911 propagation
time

There is no way to avoid the delay; any buffer drivers inserted between the Am2911 and the Am27S27 array, while they would remove the Am2911 degradation, would add a propagation delay of their own of an approximately equivalent magnitude.

The 0.1 ns/pf degradation figure is conservative, and measurements have shown that the actual degradation is somewhat less (0.07 ns/pf), but it is the accepted figure for worst case timing, where conservative estimates are desirable.

4

Refining
the CCU

In a microcomputer system there is a need to interface the main or central unit (microprocessor and/or control unit) to one or more external devices such as sensors, displays, control panels, keyboards, or external memory. The main objective is to design the interface to minimize the effect of the interface activities on the system throughput or performance. Any contact with any external device will be considered as input/output handling or I/O. Although there are many schemes for handling I/O requests, interrupts and queuing will be covered very lightly herein, principally as a means of alerting the designer to the existence of the problems. Only those schemes relevant to firmware design will be explored in any detail.

There are two very basic methods of I/O handling—status polling and interrupt servicing.

Status Polling

With status polling, the controlling unit must interrogate each peripheral to determine if it needs servicing by testing the status line of each peripheral, one at a time. This might be by the elementary "round robin" approach, where the devices are tested in a set circular sequence. Where different devices are to be handled on a priority basis,

61

priority is accomplished by assigning high-priority devices to more than one location in the testing sequence. A high priority device is tested with a higher polling frequency than the low-priority items. A flowchart of the microprogram testing sequence is shown in Figure 4-1.

The problem with status polling is that a device requesting service must wait for its turn even if all of the other devices are inactive. The controlling unit, a processor or a controller, must waste time testing inactive status lines; this reduces the possible system throughput. With the sequence test under microprogram control, a long microroutine is necessary, since each status test requires a full microinstruction. In terms of the requesting device, the system response is relatively slow.

The scheme is suitable if the frequency of service requests for each device is known with some degree of accuracy. This allows the polling frequency to be tailored to the system. The service time, once a request is acknowledged, should be long compared to the estimated wait time.

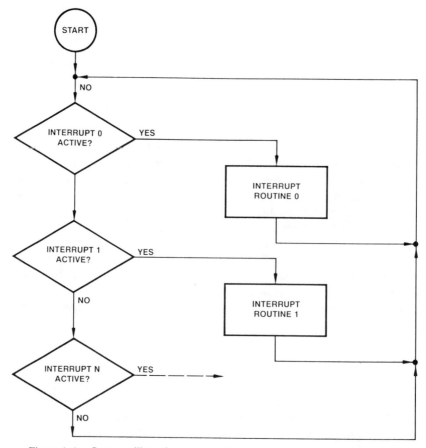

Figure 4–1.   Status polling microprogram flowchart.

It is not an advisable scheme where interfacing to a human is involved; that is, the requests should be primarily I/O to devices. (Human engineering has shown a trend in the patience level of humans to be declining from the 30 sec that was a measured average when time sharing first evolved to something much less as the user gains experience. The damage that has been done to terminals by irate users stands as mute testimony to this remark.)

Interrupt Servicing

Under interrupt servicing, the controlling unit stops to service an I/O only when an interrupt request is detected. There are two basic variations of this scheme—polled interrupt and vectored interrupt.

Polled Interrupt

With polled interrupt, all of the interrupt request lines are ORed into one interrupt request signal, and the controller tests this line periodically. Whenever a request is detected, the controller stops and then polls each device to determine which one made the request. Priority is assigned by the position a device has in the polling sequence. The overall throughput has been improved for the cases where no devices are active. However, the active device must wait while the inactive devices which proceed it in the sequence are polled.

Vectored Interrupt

With vectored interrupt, all of the device interrupt request lines are ORed as with polled interrupt. This time, when a request is sensed, the interrupt is identified to the controller. A priority scheme may or may not be involved. This scheme requires more hardware, is faster, and requires less software than the polled interrupt approach. The vectored interrupt may be thought of as a branch table, while polled interrupt is comparable to a series of IF–GO TO statements. A microprogram flowchart is given in Figure 4-2.

Implementation

There are two types of interrupt request or device service request signals—level sensitive and edge sensitive.

Level sensitive signals are generally device generated. The device raises (or lowers) its request line until the system acknowledges the signal. On receipt of the system acknowledge, the device drops its request.

Edge sensitive or pulse signals are generally initiated by a transient event occurrence. The pulse may occur one or more times and must be "caught" by the interrupt detection hardware on its first occurrence.

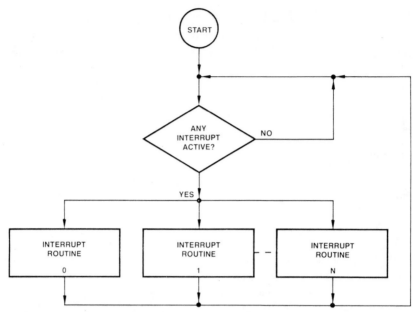

Figure 4–2.   Interrupt vectoring microprogram flowchart. One microinstruction interrupt supplies branch address for routine.

Interrupt Storage

A single interrupt store circuit involving a latch and register is shown in Figure 4-3. By setting the latch bypass control at 1 or 0 the circuit is level driven or acts as a pulse catcher.

Once the interrupt requests are clocked into the register, the register output is an interrupt request signal for the system.

Polled Interrupt

Polled interrupt would be implemented by inputting the interrupt request lines to a multiplexer and the multiplexer output to the condition test MUX of the control unit or directly into the $\overline{OE}$ of the Am2910, for example. The outputs of the register are also fed to an OR gate, which is another input to the condition test MUX. When a test is made of the OR input and it is found, e.g., an interrupt exists, a branch is made in the microprogram to an interrupt polling routine. This routine is a series of test and branch microinstructions, where each microinstruction selects one of the interrupt request lines (see Figure 4-4).

In either case, there is a limit on the number of interrupts that can be handled and a high overhead in the microword widths and the microroutine length to provide for the desired number of allowable interrupts.

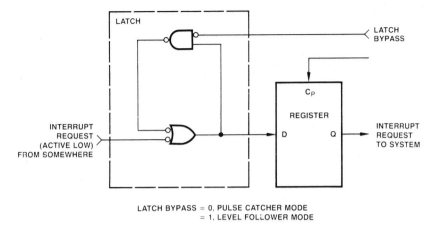

LATCH BYPASS = 0, PULSE CATCHER MODE
= 1, LEVEL FOLLOWER MODE

Figure 4–3.   Single interrupt storage. Latch bypass = 0, pulse catcher; = 1, level driven.

Vectored Interrupt

With vectored interrupt, an OR gate is still involved and still feeds into one input of the conditional test MUX. However, the interrupt or device identification is provided to the system without further demands on the available MUX inputs.

One scheme for identification of the interrupt is to use a priority encoder such as the Am2913. This device accepts eight interrupts (active low) and outputs a 3 bit vector, which is the binary index of the highest priority interrupt line. It also outputs a fourth signal, which is the OR gate, i.e., ANY. The logical block is shown in Figure 4-5.

The index itself is a partial address, and there are various schemes that could be used. Two are considered here.

The 3 bits could be a complete start address, with zeros driven into low-order bit locations. This fixes the areas within the microprogram memory where the start addresses of the appropriate service routines may be placed.

The 3 bits could be a complete address into the lower address portion of the micromemory, with an interrupt jump table stored there. This frees the routine to be placed anywhere but requires that the first few words of the micromemory be reserved for the jump table.

Vector Mapping PROM

Rather than using the main microprogram memory to store a branch table, which requires a full microword to store what is essentially a branch address, it is better to use a vector mapping PROM. A vector mapping PROM is similar to the mapping PROM that was used earlier for the start addresses of the normal microroutines, with the vector mapping PROM providing the start addresses of interrupt service microroutines.

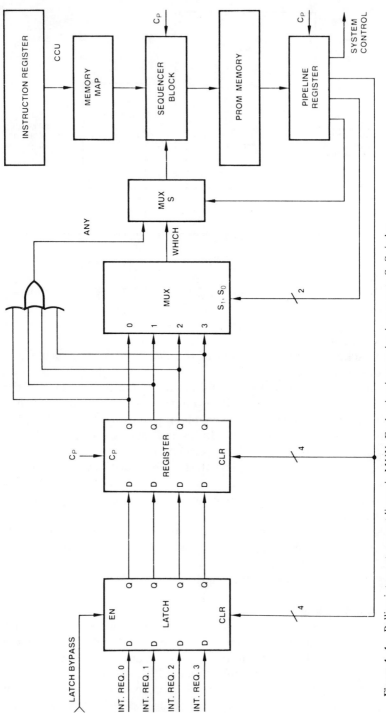

Figure 4–4.   Polling interrupt request lines via MUX. Each microinstruction increments S_1 S_0 index to examine next request line.

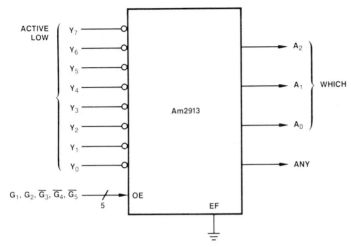

Figure 4-5. Am2913 priority interrupt encoder/expander (limited!). If Y_7 low, output is $(111)_2$, all other Y_i are "don't care." A_2 A_1 A_0 represents index of highest priority interrupt received. This is the address or address modifier for the service routine.

The index bits from the priority encoder are the address bits supplied to the vector mapping PROM, and the PROM output is a full n-bit address. By using a PROM with tristate output as the vector map, the map can share the microprogram address input with the mapping PROM and the branch address. The next-address control block must supply an $\overline{OE}_{vector}$ control line in this case (see Figure 4-6).

Next-Address Control

The next-address control can be handled by an Am29811A and an Am25LS139 decoder. $\overline{OE}_{map}$ and $\overline{OE}_{pipeline}$ are supplied by the Am29811A. By inputting these signals to the decoder, the three required output enable signals are generated. The Am29811 has an instruction called CJV (Conditional Jump Vector), which operates as any of the other conditional instructions except that if COND. = TRUE, the vector map is enabled and $\overline{OE}_{map}$ and $\overline{OE}_{pipeline}$ are used to disable the mapping PROM and the pipeline register.

If the microprogram sequencer which was developed in Chapter 3 is modified by making the register and the counter into one unit with the associated next-address control changes, then the register/counter, next-address logic, the next-address MUX, the stack, the TOS pointer, the μPC register, and the incrementer exist as a single IC device. This is the Am2910 microprogram controller, which can address up to 4K of PROM memory. It is approximately equivalent to three Am2911s, an Am29811, and an Am25LS139. It is referred to as the "supersequencer" and is powerful enough for most controller applications (see Figure 4-7). The condition MUX, polarity block, and pipeline registers for the instructions to these devices exist as the Am2922.

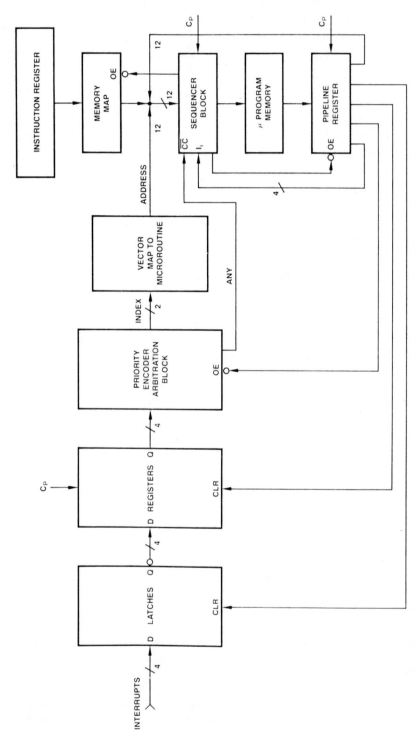

Figure 4–6.   Using a vector map.

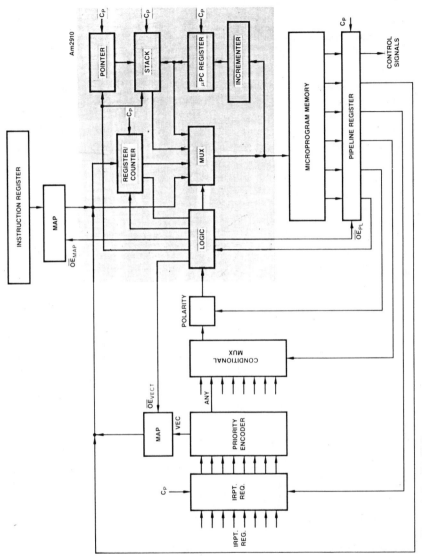

Figure 4–7. Am2910 supersequencer.

Am2910

The block diagram of the Am2910 is shown in Figure 4-8. This device is controlled by a 4-bit instruction, which would be supplied from one field of the microword format of the system. These four bits provide 16 basic instructions, which are similar to but not identical with the Am29811A instructions. They are discussed in detail in this chapter.

The Am2910 can address up to 4K of PROM/ROM memory. Unused address lines are left floating at the output; the corresponding D_i inputs should be tied to ground. It provides three output enable controls: $\overline{PL}$,

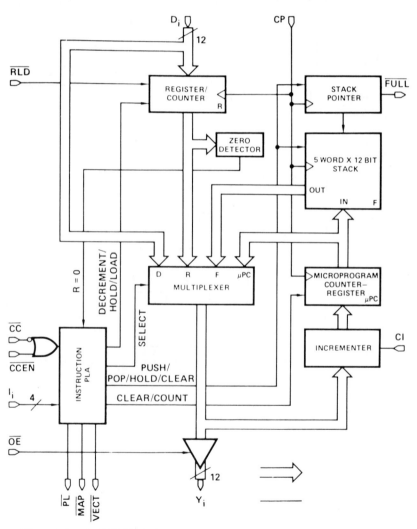

Figure 4–8.   Am2910 block diagram.

$\overline{\text{MAP}}$, and $\overline{\text{VECT}}$. The 4 bit instruction, the result of the $\overline{\text{CC}}$, $\overline{\text{CCEN}}$ inputs, and the internal zero detect for the register/counter all are inputs to an onboard instruction PLA (programmable logic array). The PLA provides the internal controls which correspond to the next-address control logic. The next address can be from one of four sources: (1) the microprogram counter (μPC), (2) the LIFO stack (F), (3) the register/counter (R), or direct input (D), from whatever is connected to the D_i inputs. D_i is connected to the tristated outputs of the vector map, the mapping PROM, and the pipeline in the example CCU developed so far.

Am2910 Instructions

Jump Zero (JZ)

Power up or restart sequences need to use the Jump Zero instruction if the stack is to be used anywhere in the microprogram. JZ resets the TOS pointer to binary 0. JZ may be made to execute in various ways.

If a pipeline is being used, resetting the pipeline register to all zero sends 0_{16} as the hex code for the instruction word. Since $0_{16} = $ JZ, the Am2910 executes JZ. A reset, restart, or power up control should cause the pipeline to reset.

Where the pipeline on the PROM memory does not exist, the $\overline{\text{OE}}$ control on the Am2910 can be used with 10K pull-up resistors to force FFF_{16} on the address lines into the PROM memory. The JZ instruction should be placed at this location. This approach requires an extra microword in the memory, which is not usually a problem. Either of these approaches is satisfactory.

JZ does not alter the register/counter, which is assumed to be undefined until reset. Any reference to the register/counter prior to a load instruction will result in unpredictable behavior.

The pipeline is left enabled in this instruction. With the exceptions of instructions JMAP and CJV, the pipeline is left enabled to improve execution speeds. A flow diagram for JZ is shown in Figure 4-9.

All instructions pass the next-address select bits, which include the Am2910 instruction field, the condition code multiplexer select bits, and any additional control pin fields ($\overline{\text{RLD}}$, $\overline{\text{CCEN}}$). All instructions cause a next-address value to be switched through the next-address multiplexer and to be incremented by the incrementer.

Continue (CONT)

Sequential program segments use the Continue statement, whose flow is shown in Figure 4-10. The micro-PC register is the source of the next-address. The register/counter and the stack are not altered; the $\overline{\text{CC}}$ input is unused. The pipeline output enable $\overline{\text{PL}}$ is enabled.

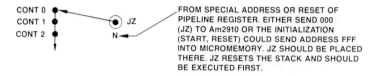

CONT 0
CONT 1
CONT 2

JZ

N

FROM SPECIAL ADDRESS OR RESET OF
PIPELINE REGISTER. EITHER SEND 000
(JZ) TO Am2910 OR THE INITIALIZATION
(START, RESET) COULD SEND ADDRESS FFF
INTO MICROMEMORY. JZ SHOULD BE PLACED
THERE. JZ RESETS THE STACK AND SHOULD
BE EXECUTED FIRST.

$\overline{CC}$	COUNTER = 0 LINE	STACK	ADDRESS SOURCE	REGISTER/ COUNTER	$\overline{OE}$
X	X	CLEAR	0	NC	PL

Figure 4–9. Jump zero (JZ, 0).

Jump Map (JMAP)

The instruction used to start different microroutines based on op code decode, and a mapping PROM or the equivalent construct, is JMAP. This GO TO branches to the address appearing at the D_i inputs, and the $\overline{MAP}$ output enable is active. In a CCU such as the one being discussed, this will gate the address output by the mapping PROM into the Am2910. The register/counter and stack are not affected. This statement is normally located at the end of a microroutine or placed at a case-branch (jump-op) location in the microprogram (see Figure 4-11).

Conditional Jump PL (CJP)

The simplest IF construct is the Conditional Jump to an address in the pipeline register. The jump is made if the $\overline{CC}$ input is LOW (condition true). If the $\overline{CC}$ input is HIGH, the test fails and CJP behaves as a

CONT 50
CONT 51
CONT 52
CONT 53

SEQUENTIAL
PROGRAM
FLOW

$\overline{CC}$	COUNTER = 0 LINE	STACK	ADDRESS SOURCE	REGISTER/ COUNTER	$\overline{OE}$
X	X	NC	μPC	NC	PL

Figure 4–10. Continue (CONT, E).

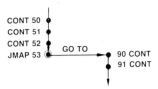

$\overline{CC}$	COUNTER = 0 LINE	STACK	ADDRESS SOURCE	REGISTER/ COUNTER	$\overline{OE}$
X	X	NC	D	NC	MAP

Figure 4–11.   Jump map (JMAP, 2).

CONT instruction. The pipeline is enabled and the register and stack are unaffected (see Figure 4-12).

Conditional Jump Vector (CJV)

The IF construct used to test for the occurrence of an interrupt request is Conditional Jump Vector. If the $\overline{CC}$ input is low, the next address is provided by the vector map. The stack and register counter are unaffected. The VECT enable is active. If $\overline{CC}$ is high, CJV behaves as CONT (see Figure 4-13).

Load Counter and Continue (LDCT)

There are a number of instructions which use the counter capability and several which use the register capability of the register/counter. Each requires that the register/counter be loaded prior to its execution. Load Counter and Continue provides this ability. LDCT behaves as a

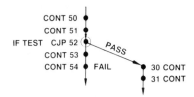

$\overline{CC}$	COUNTER = 0 LINE	STACK	ADDRESS SOURCE	REGISTER/ COUNTER	$\overline{OE}$
PASS FAIL	X	NC	D μPC	NC	PL

Figure 4–12.   Conditional jump pipeline (CJP, 3).

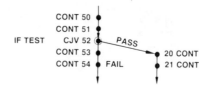

$\overline{CC}$	COUNTER = 0 LINE	STACK	ADDRESS SOURCE	REGISTER/ COUNTER	$\overline{OE}$
PASS FAIL	X	NC	D μPC	NC	VECT

Figure 4–13.   Conditional jump vector (CJV, 6).

continue statement except that whatever is gated on the D_i inputs is *unconditionally* loaded into the register/counter. The $\overline{PL}$ enable is active; the stack is unaffected (see Figure 4-14).

COND Jump R/PL (JRP)

The Conditional Jump Register/Pipeline should actually have been given the mnemonic CJRP. (The mnemonic names refer to the Development System, AmSYS 29, preprogrammed Definition File.) The choice of where the next address comes from is made based on the $\overline{CC}$ input. If $\overline{CC}$ is LOW, the next address is from the pipeline. If $\overline{CC}$ is HIGH, the next address is from the register/counter. LDCT or an equivalent operation *must have occurred anywhere prior* to JRP. Regardless of the result of the test, the flow is nonsequential. The $\overline{PL}$

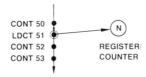

$\overline{CC}$	COUNTER = 0 LINE	STACK	ADDRESS SOURCE	REGISTER/ COUNTER	$\overline{OE}$
X	X	NC	μPC	LOAD	PL

Figure 4–14.   Load counter and continue (LDCT, C). This instruction must be executed before a loop instruction or a jump which used the register.

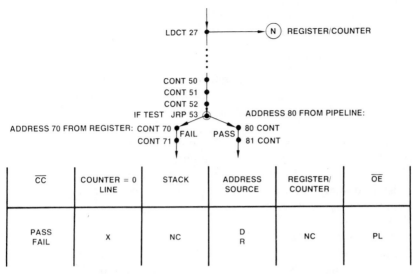

Figure 4–15. Conditional jump register/pipeline (JRP, 7). LDCT must have been executed somewhere ahead of JRP.

enable is active, and the register/counter and the stack are unaffected (see Figure 4-15).

COND JSB PL (CJS)
Microprogram subroutines may be called by Conditional Jump Subroutine with the address of the first microinstruction of the subroutine given in the pipeline register. If $\overline{CC}$ is LOW, a branch is taken to the subroutine. The contents of the μPC, which on the flow diagram of Figure 4-16 is address 53, are pushed onto the stack and the TOS pointer

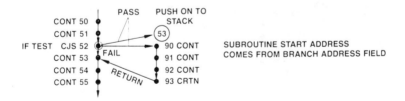

Figure 4–16. Conditional jump subroutine from pipeline (CJS, 1).

is incremented. If $\overline{CC}$ is high, CJS behaves as CONT. The $\overline{PL}$ enable is active; the register/counter is unaffected.

COND JSB R/PL (JSRP)

Subroutines may also be called by a Conditional Jump Subroutine from Register or Pipeline, which should actually have been given the mnemonic CSRP. The instruction is similar to JRP except that regardless of the test result the next sequential address (55 in Figure 4-17) is pushed onto the stack and the TOS pointer is incremented. As with JRP, LDCT or an equivalent operation *must have occurred prior* to JSRP. If $\overline{CC}$ is LOW, the subroutine start address is taken from the register/counter. The $\overline{PL}$ enable is active; the register/counter is unaffected.

COND Return (CRTN)

Once a subroutine has been completed, an unconditional return to the calling program is accomplished using a Conditional Return Statement. The conditional return is also used to conditionally end a subroutine based on the result of a test.

There are two ways to allow an unconditional return—either the selected input to the conditional MUX is a forced PASS input (grounded in the active low case), or the $\overline{CCEN}$ input is switched high. $\overline{CCEN}$ will be discussed later. If $\overline{CC}$ is LOW either as a result of a valid test or

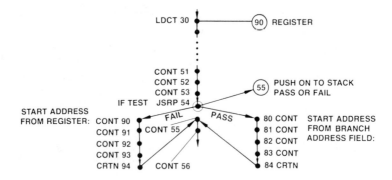

$\overline{\overline{CC}}$	COUNTER = 0 LINE	STACK	ADDRESS SOURCE	REGISTER/ COUNTER	$\overline{OE}$
PASS FAIL	X	PUSH	D R	NC	PL

Figure 4–17. Conditional jump subroutine register/pipeline (JSRP, 5). LDCT or a register load must occur somewhere prior to JSRP.

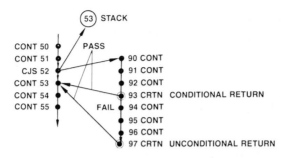

$\overline{CC}$	COUNTER = 0 LINE	STACK	ADDRESS SOURCE	REGISTER/ COUNTER	$\overline{OE}$
PASS FAIL	X	POP NC	STACK μPC	NC	PL
DISABLE ($\overline{CCEN}$ = H OR $\overline{CC}$ = L)	X	POP	STACK	NC	PL

Figure 4–18.   Conditional return (CRTN, A).

from a forced low input, the next address is taken from the LIFO stack and the stack is POPped (the TOS pointer is decremented). The register/counter is unaffected, and the $\overline{PL}$ enable is active.

If $\overline{CC}$ is HIGH, CRTN behaves as CONT. In either case, CRTN should not be executed if the stack is empty (see Figure 4-18).

Repeat PL CNTR $\neq$ 0 (RPCT)

Loops are handled with four different instructions. One of these is the RPCT Repeat Loop instruction, with the start address of the loop in the pipeline register. Essentially it is a conditional jump pipeline instruction. The register/counter must have been loaded previously via a LDCT or equivalent operation. If the counter is not equal to 0, the jump is taken and the counter is decremented. If <COUNTER> = 0, then RPCT behaves as CONT. The stack is unaffected, and the $\overline{PL}$ enable is active (see Figure 4-19).

Push/COND LD CNTR (PUSH)

The counter can be conditionally loaded during the same instruction that pushes the current value of the μPC register onto the LIFO stack. If $\overline{CC}$ is LOW, the counter is loaded from the pipeline register. If $\overline{CC}$ is HIGH, the register/counter is unchanged. The PUSH occurs regardless of the $\overline{CC}$ input value. The PL enable is active (see Figure 4-20). PUSH must immediately precede the first microinstruction in a loop controlled by LOOP, RFCT, or TWB.

Repeat Loop, CNTR $\neq$ 0 (RFCT)

Another Repeat Loop structure is RFCT, which causes a loop to be repeated if <COUNTER> $\neq$ 0. The start address of the loop is on the

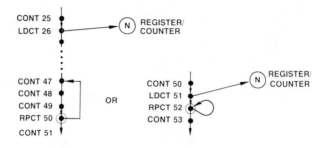

$\overline{CC}$	COUNTER = 0 LINE	STACK	ADDRESS SOURCE	REGISTER/ COUNTER	$\overline{OE}$
X	=0 ≠0 (PART OF INSTR. PLA)	NC	μPC D	NC DECREMENT	PL

Figure 4–19.   Repeat pipeline if counter ≠ 0 (RPCT, 9). (Loop on one or more statements, beginning address of loop in pipeline [at RPCT statement].)

top of the stack. The counter is decremented when the branch is taken. If <COUNTER> = 0, RFCT behaves similarly to CONT with the added operation of popping the stack. The $\overline{PL}$ enable is active. A loop using RFCT requires PUSH immediately preceding the first microinstruction of the loop, the microinstruction whose address is to be pushed onto the stack (see Figure 4-21). RPCT and RFCT are both microprogramming equivalents of DO loops.

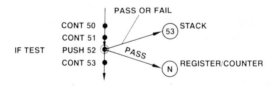

$\overline{CC}$	COUNTER = 0 LINE	STACK	ADDRESS SOURCE	REGISTER/ COUNTER	$\overline{OE}$
PASS FAIL	X	PUSH	μPC	LOAD NC	PL

Figure 4–20.   Push stack and conditional load counter (PUSH, 4). This instruction must immediately precede the first statement in a loop controlled by LOOP or RFCT.

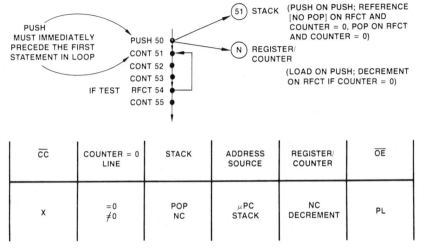

Figure 4–21.   Repeat loop from stack if counter ≠ 0 (RFCT, 8).

Test End Loop (LOOP)

A third repeat loop construct is LOOP, which behaves similarly to RFCT except that the test which determines whether or not the loop is repeated is some selected condition other than <COUNTER> = 0. On $\overline{CC}$ = HIGH, LOOP behaves similarly to CONT, with the added operation of popping the stack. On $\overline{CC}$ = LOW, the loop start address is referenced from the top of the stack. The register/counter is unaffected. The $\overline{PL}$ enable is active.

A loop using the instruction LOOP requires that PUSH immediately precede the first microinstruction, the one whose address is to be pushed onto the stack (see Figure 4-22).

LOOP is a microprogramming equivalent of a DO UNTIL or DO WHILE loop.

COND JUMP PL and POP (CJPP)

The way to conditionally exit a loop is to execute CJPP. This instruction may also be used to conditionally exit a subroutine where a return to the calling location is to be aborted.

CJPP is a conditional jump using the pipeline register to provide the branch address (see Figure 4-23). The difference between CJP and CJPP is that the latter pops the stack when $\overline{CC}$ = LOW. When $\overline{CC}$ = HIGH, CJPP behaves as CONT. The $\overline{PL}$ enable is active.

CJPP is used to conditionally exit loops formed using PUSH and RFCT, TWB, or LOOP. It is not needed for loops formed with RPCT which do not involve the stack.

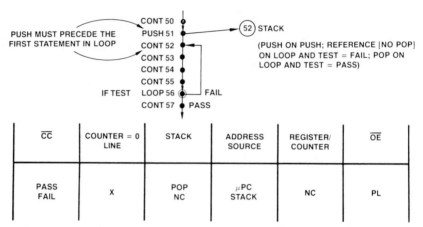

$\overline{CC}$	COUNTER = 0 LINE	STACK	ADDRESS SOURCE	REGISTER/ COUNTER	$\overline{OE}$
PASS FAIL	X	POP NC	μPC STACK	NC	PL

Figure 4–22.   Test end of loop (LOOP, D). Must be preceding first statement in loop.

Three-Way Branch (TWB)

There can be instances where the construct DO X TIMES WHILE C_i = FALSE is necessary. The microinstruction equivalent of this is TWB, a dual-test branch or loop microinstruction (see Figure 4-24).

TWB will loop, referring to the top of the stack for the start address, if $\overline{CC}$ = HIGH *and* <COUNTER> ≠ 0. The stack will be POPped on the branch if CC = HIGH and <COUNTER> = 0. TWB will behave similarly to CONT if $\overline{CC}$ = LOW with the addition of popping the stack, regardless of the counter value. If <COUNTER> ≠ 0, the counter will be decremented. In all cases, the $\overline{PL}$ enable is active.

An example of the type of problem for which TWB is useful is given in Figure 4-25. This is a key match memory search, where the counter defines the length of the block of memory being searched and the condition tested is a match on the selected key.

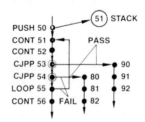

$\overline{CC}$	COUNTER = 0 LINE	STACK	ADDRESS SOURCE	REGISTER/ COUNTER	$\overline{OE}$
PASS FAIL	X	POP NC	D μPC	NC	PL

Figure 4–23.   Conditional jump pipeline and POP (CJPP, B).

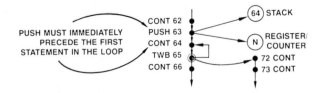

$\overline{CC}$	COUNTER = 0 LINE	STACK	ADDRESS SOURCE	REGISTER/ COUNTER	$\overline{OE}$
PASS	=0 ≠0	POP	μPC	NC DECREMENT	PL
FAIL	=0 ≠0	POP NC	D STACK	NC DECREMENT	

Figure 4–24.   Three-way branch (TWB, F).

Control Lines

In addition to the four instruction lines, there are additional control lines which allow variations in the instructions.

Register Load

The $\overline{RLD}$ pin is the register load control pin and is normally held high. When $\overline{RLD}$ = LOW, whatever is on the D_i bus is loaded into the register/counter. The $\overline{RLD}$ pin allows the Continue (CONT) instruction

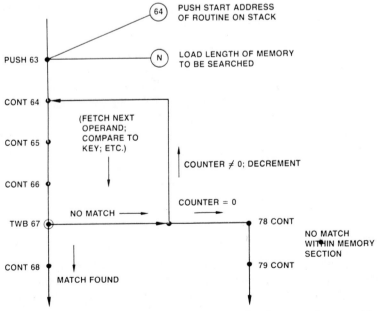

Figure 4–25.   Programming a memory search on key for a search on $n + 1$ locations.

to become Load Register and Continue, the same as the existing LDCT. It also allows a Jump Map (JMAP) to become Load Register and Jump Map, which could be useful if fail-soft procedures are desirable. (Selected instructions could be reexecuted on recovery.)

It could also lead to problems. Misuse, such as holding $\overline{\text{RLD}}$ low during Repeat Loop from Pipeline Until <COUNTER> = 0 (RPCT), could lead to infinite loops. $\overline{\text{RLD}}$ should not be low during any instruction loop where the counter or register is being used. This includes RFCT, RPCT, and TWB loops.

Test Enable
The test pin, $\overline{\text{CC}}$ (active low), is the input from the conditional test MUX, an Am2914, or other structure. All conditional instructions reference this pin. The test enable $\overline{\text{CCEN}}$, if held high, causes all conditional instructions to become unconditional instructions, behaving as if the $\overline{\text{CC}}$ input were LOW (condition = true) and forcing the appropriate jump. This affects nine instructions; see Table 4-1.

$\overline{\text{CCEN}}$ can be supplied by the microinstruction or could be tied to one of the instruction lines into the Am2910.

Carry In
There is a C_{in} pin which is normally held high. When C_{in} = LOW the incrementer does not increment, holding the microprogram in a one-statement loop. To avoid infinite looping, the C_{in} pin, if controlled, must *not* be controlled via the pipeline register; it must be controlled by independent hardware. The C_{in} pin can be used to hold a program at NOP or a similar instruction until some external signal triggers the control circuit.

Stack and Enable
There is a five-deep stack on board the Am2910 which, unlike the Am2909/11 stack, will not "wrap around." The behavior of the Am2910 *should be considered to be undefined under stack misuse*. A pin is provided that can be used during initial design and/or debug which allows the stack to be tested. $\overline{\text{FULL}}$ goes low to indicate when five items have been pushed onto the stack without any pops.

The tristated control $\overline{\text{OE}}$ pin allows the Am2910 to share a bus with other devices, including other Am2910s.

Interrupt Handling

In a computer system, the minimal storage required for the system to be able to resume operations after handling an interrupt would provide the ability to store the PC register and the PSW, which includes

Table 4–1   Effect of $\overline{\text{CCEN}}$ = HIGH

Original Instructions	Behavior	New Instructions
CJP	Jump to pipeline	JPL
CJPP	Jump pipeline and pop stack	JPP
CJS	Jump to subroutine	JSUB
CJV	Jump vector	JVECT
CRTN	Return	RTRN
JSRP	Jump to subroutine (same)	JSUB
LOOP	POP stack and continue	POP
PUSH	PUSH, load counter, and continue	PCNTR
TWB	POP stack and continue (same)	POP

the ACC register and the status bits. More complicated systems require additional storage, such as the storage of the current stack pointer, scratchpad registers, and all other machine registers. Nested interrupts are handled in software by stack operations and subroutine call procedures. Enable/disable capability and clear interrupt mechanisms are essential. Clear interrupts can be clear one, clear several, or clear all current interrupts in a system. Refer to Figure 4-26 for the flow of interrupt handling via software; it is seen to be markedly identical to subroutine handling.

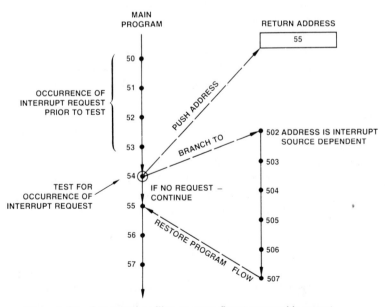

Figure 4–26.   Interrupt handling program flow (recoverable status).

Clearing Interrupts

To be able to clear the current interrupt using the interrupt hardware developed earlier, the vector map index generated by the priority encoder must be brought out to flip-flops for storage. A control bit from the pipeline will cause the actual storage operation. The flip-flops feed a decoder, which is enabled under pipeline control. When the decoder output is enabled, it drives the clear lines into the latches and the interrupt registers.

Interrupt Enable

Occasionally it is desirable to block one or more interrupts during a program, such as (1) when a peripheral is "down," (2) when a unit is under on-line test, (3) when selective testing is underway, or (4) when high priority software is being executed. Bit masking allows any one, several, or all interrupts at any level or levels to be blocked.

Bit masking can be added to the control being constructed by adding a loadable mask register which will block all masked bits from being input to the priority encoder or from triggering the interrupt request line.

Nested Interrupts

Nested interrupts behave as nested subroutine calls, as shown in the flow diagram of Figure 4-27. Where multilevel interrupts can exist, a higher priority interrupt must be able to interrupt a lower level one. In a microprogram controlled interrupt system, the presence of an interrupt is tested for by a conditional test statement such as CJP or CJS. The test should be made at a quiescent point in the microroutine, usually where the stack activity is low and the counter/register is not in use. No interrupts should be tested for within a loop or a subroutine nest. Care must be exercised to prevent the stack from overflowing.

Status Fence

To implement a nested interrupt capability, a status fence is required. Because there is a particular device in mind, this is shown in Figure 4-28 to consist of: (1) an incrementer to increment the current vector index being generated by the priority encoder, (2) a loadable status register to hold the current "fence" value, and (3) a comparator to compare the loaded status (always greater than the one in service) and the current vector index being generated. The comparator will generate a signal when the incoming interrupt is equal to or greater than the current status. This signal will be NANDed with the interrupt signals from the unmasked interrupts to generate an active low signal to be input to the $\overline{CC}$ pin of the Am2910 or to a condition MUX input pin. Also, the comparator output enables tristate buffers that control the output of the actual interrupt vector index to the vector map.

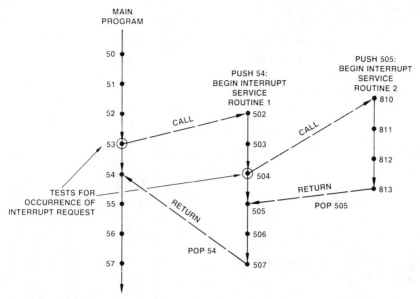

Figure 4–27. Nested interrupt flow (recoverable status). Recovery of addresses same as nested subroutines.

Other Embellishments

To recover from an interrupt or to unwind an interrupt nest, the status and mask registers must be readable (so that they can be saved) as well as loadable (so that they can be restored). The control should be able to use the mask register or mask register input bus to selectively clear some or all interrupts to expand interrupt clear capability.

Am2914

The Am2914 (see Figure 4-29) incorporates all of these desired features. It contains (1) the latches, (2) mask register, (3) status fence register, (4) priority encoder, (5) vector hold register, (6) clear control, (7) incrementer, (8) comparator, and (9) interconnection logic for expansion. One device handles up to eight interrupt sources.

The instruction set for the Am2914 is shown in Table 4-2, and a program flow is shown in Figure 4-30 which diagrams where, within a microprogram structure, the various Am2914 instructions could appear.

Interconnection of the Am2914

Single Unit

The Am2914 requires that the status overflow pin be connected to the interrupt disable pin. The GAR and GEN pins are grounded; GAS,

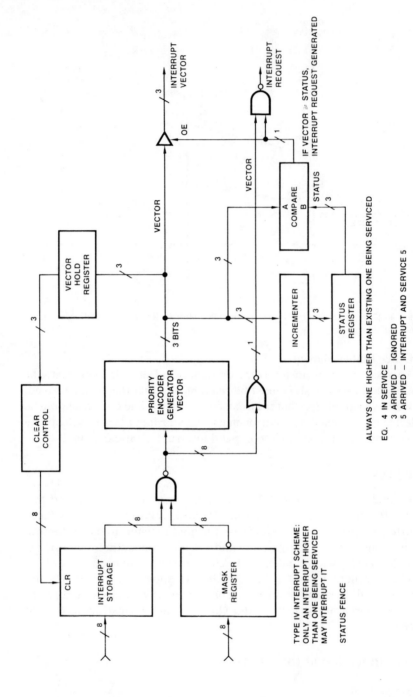

Figure 4–28. Clear control, status fence, and bit marking for interrupt controller.

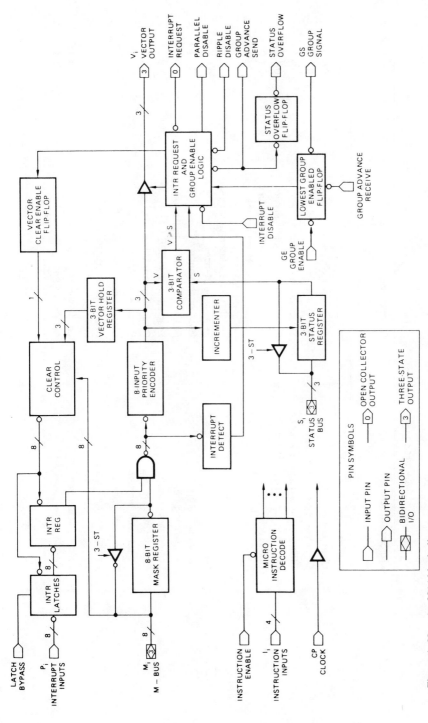

Figure 4-29. Am2914 block diagram.

Table 4-2 Am2914 Instruction Set

Microinstruction	Description	Microcode $I_3 I_2 I_1 I_0$
Master clear	Initialize	0 0 0 0
Clear all interrupts	All latches, registers	0 0 0 1
Clear interrupts from M-bus	Selective clear	0 0 1 0
Clear interrupts from mask register	Selective clear (M-bus floating)	0 0 1 1
Clear interrupts, last vector read	Specific clear or clear on service	0 1 0 0
Read vector	—Read vector of highest priority interrupt requesting service	0 1 0 1
	—Sets status fence	
	—Sets up clear last instruction	
Read status register	Read status fence	0 1 1 0
Read mask register	Read enable pattern	0 1 1 1
Set mask register	Bits where M-bus = 1 affected	1 0 0 0
Load status register	Load status and LGE F/F	1 0 0 1
Bit clear mask register	Clear bit where M-bus = 1	1 0 1 0
Bit set mask register	Set bit where M-bus = 1	1 0 1 1
Clear mask register	Clear all bits	1 1 0 0
Disable interrupt request	Disable interrupts and reset interrupt request enable F/F	1 1 0 1
Load mask register	Load entire register	1 1 1 0
Enable interrupt request	Set enable F/F	1 1 1 1

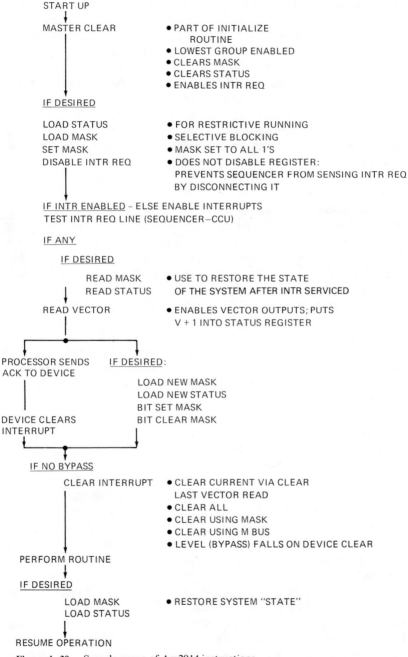

Figure 4–30. Sample usage of Am2914 instructions.

GSIG, RDIS, and PDIS are left floating. When the highest priority interrupt is reached, the interrupt controller is disabled until a new status is loaded or a master clear is executed. The highest level interrupt should be reserved for catastrophic occurrences.

For all other status levels, when a higher status is to be executed, and recovery is desired, the existing status should be read so that it may be reloaded upon completion of the higher level interrupt, if another higher level interrupt has not occurred in the interim. Care should be taken to eliminate or reduce cycles in status read and load operations. (Possibly a decrementing of the current status and check on interrupts is a better unwinding procedure.)

Interconnection

To interconnect a single Am2914 to the microsystem, the Am2914 must receive four instruction bits and an instruction enable bit from the pipeline register. The 16-bit system data bus would be used to supply the 3-bit status read/load lines and the 8-bit mask read/load lines. The vector output would feed the vector mapping PROM or other decode unit, which in turn would connect to the 16-bit data bus. The eight interrupt request lines would be connected to whatever interrupts are to be allowed in the proper priority sequence. The interrupt request line is tied high through 470Ω and inputs to either the $\overline{CC}$ input of the Am2910 or some similar connection. This provides an 8-level interrupt control system (see Figure 4-31). A 16-level interconnect is shown in Figure 4-32 using an Am2913 expander; 64-level systems are demonstrated in the AMD application note.

Microprogram Interrupt

The Am2914 interrupt controller may be interconnected to provide a microprogram level interrupt system or a machine program interrupt system. In the former, the microcode would contain tests for the occurrence of any interrupt at "quiet" points in the microcode. These are placed where the subroutine stack is empty, such as at the end of the microroutine for an op code or between modules within a very long microroutine. The response to the interrupt is relatively fast; the op code itself is unchanged, but it does require additional control memory storage.

The occurrence of an interrupt would cause a branch address to be input to the PROM/ROM (through the Am2910 or Am2911s), which in turn would cause the interrupt service microroutine to begin executing. The end of this service microroutine would cause either a return to the interrupted op code microroutine or a JMAP to fetch the next op code. The interrupt routine could be called by a simple conditional jump or by a conditional jump to subroutine. A controller using an Am2910, and Am2914 is shown in Figure 4-33.

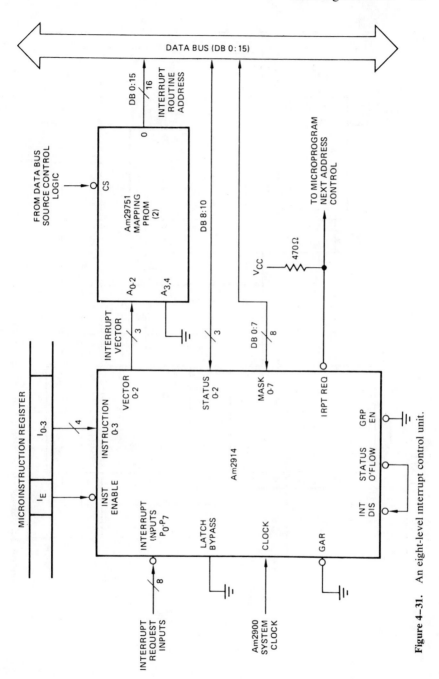

Figure 4-31. An eight-level interrupt control unit.

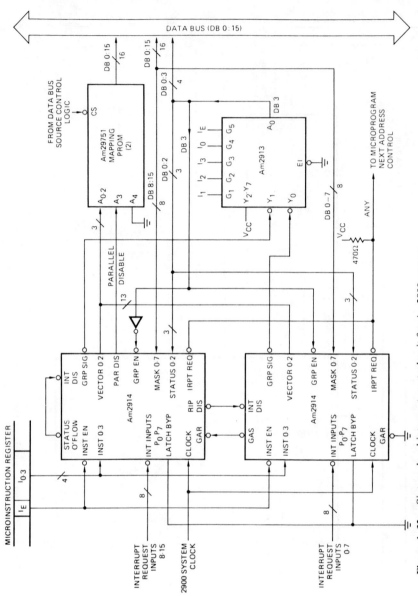

Figure 4–32.   Sixteen-level interrupt control unit for Am2900 system.

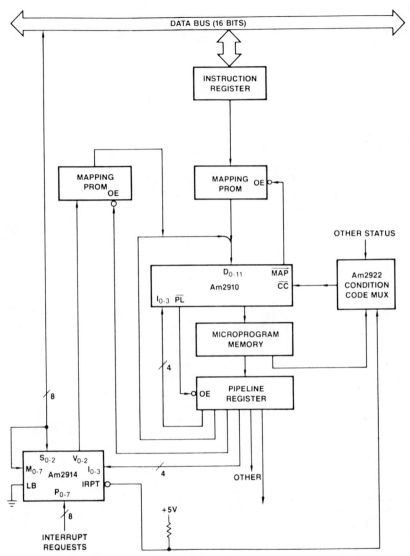

Figure 4–33. Computer control unit for microprogram interrupt system.

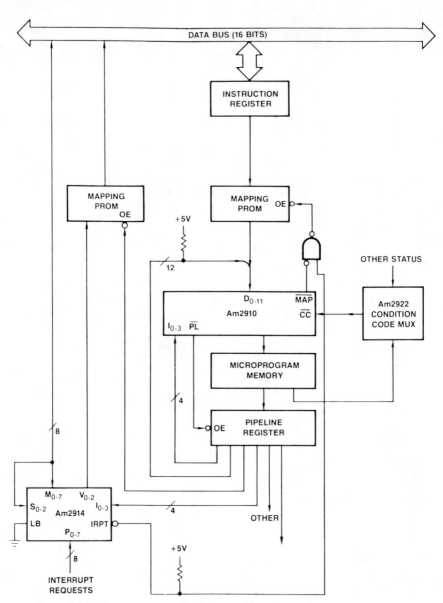

Figure 4–34. Computer control unit for machine program interrupt system.

Machine Level Interrupt

A machine program interrupt system may test for an interrupt only at the *end* of the microroutine for the current op code since the contents of the instruction register will be destroyed. The existence of an interrupt in this case would cause the vector map to output to the system data bus.

Two procedures could exist. In the first, the vector map output could in fact be a special op code, fed into the instruction register and handled as any other op code. The microroutine for this special op code would exist in the PROM memory, and a start address would exist for the microroutine in the memory map. This is a relatively fast procedure but requires space for the op codes and a larger control memory.

In the second, the vector map output would be processed by system software and would be used to call up a machine level interrupt program. The program would be executed as any other software program. This is a relatively slow interrupt service procedure, with the advantages of having no additional microprogram PROM requirements and requiring no additional map space.

A computer control unit for machine program interrupt handling is shown in Figure 4-34, constructed from an Am2910 and two Am2914s. Note that this version does not require a decoder for the output enable of the memory map. As shown, the $\overline{OE}_{vect}$ must come from the microword just as the instruction register load control and other system controls.

5

Evolution
of the ALU

The basic controller is well defined at this point in the design. If a CCU is being developed, the next step is the development of an appropriate ALU and the other related modules which will comprise the CPU of the system as well as the interconnect to the main read–write system memory.

Instruction Formats

The simple ALU shown in Figure 5-1 has (1) an ALU, with carry in and function control coming from the CCU, and (2) an ACC register, with load enable control coming from the CCU. This simple system could support ADD, SUB, OR, EXOR, LOAD ACC, or PASS. The assumption was made that data came in only on the A port of the ALU and therefore that the instruction had the form:

Op Code	Operand Address

Single address instruction

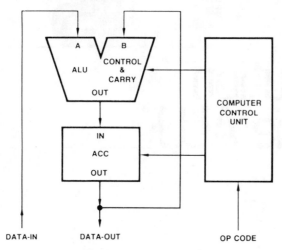

Figure 5–1. Simple system.

This is only one of many forms that could occur among various systems or within any one system.

There are often several formats for instructions in a system, of which some of the more typical for direct addressing are

—op code with implied operand
—op code with single address
—op code with two addresses
—op code with three addresses

Literals, indexed registers, indirect addresses, base relative addresses, register addresses, and combinations of these are ignored here.

Control Unit Function

As a computer control, the CCU must be able to direct the fetch of the op code to the instruction register and decode whether or not part of the instruction contains an address. If it does, that address must be gated into the MAR, which will then be used to fetch the actual data from memory. In the simple system being described, the op code will be gated into the IR (instruction register) at the same time that the address is gated into the MAR.

If a memory fetch for data is required, the decode of the op code will produce the required microinstructions to perform the actual fetch. Once all of the operands are available, the ALU function execution proceeds. In the simple system being described, the fetch of the second operand occurs in the same microcycle as the ALU execute.

PC and MAR

Involved in the above memory fetch operations are two registers, the PC and the MAR. The PC (program counter) stores the address of the next machine level (macro) instruction to be fetched from the program area of main memory. The MAR (memory address register) contains the address which is to be placed on the main memory address bus. The address will be either that transferred from the PC register (instruction fetch) or that loaded from an instruction (data fetch). In the SIMCOM (simple computer) system, only the MAR connects to the address bus, although both the PC and MAR could be used to supply an address to the memory, at the cost of increased complexity in the bus structure. Both the PC and the MAR are loaded from the ALU output as shown in Figure 5-2.

Now assume that the program is executing an arithmetic ADD and that address i is in the PC register. This is the address of the next instruction to be fetched (see Figure 5-3). The PC register contents are placed on the main memory address bus via the MAR, and the contents at address i are fetched and loaded into the instruction register (IR) and the MAR.

The MAR register contents (address j) are placed on the memory address bus under the control of the CCU and the contents of the storage location at address j are fetched and input to the data input part of the ALU.

At the same time, the ACC passes its contents to the other part of the ALU and the CCU sends a control instruction to the ALU. These three events are coordinated so that the two operands arrive at the same instant $I \pm t_e$ (t_e is some allowable error, some unit of time). The ALU is ready to process them when they arrive. On the next clock, the result is loaded into the ACC. The PC is incremented and execution continues.

The design in Figure 5-2 uses the ALU to increment the PC register and could place the result either in the PC register or in both the PC and MAR registers. The MAR cannot input to the PC register in this configuration.

Also shown is a connection to the ACC outputs such that the test for $<ACC> = 0$ is possible. There are no other status outputs for the ALU as yet. The test input is connected to the CCU, which is at the moment considered to be an undefined black box.

With this design, the SIMCOM supports a basic instruction set that includes basic arithmetic and logical operations as well as some memory access and branch instructions, as summarized in Table 5-1. INA and OUT allow data to come into or be placed out of the system, via the data bus, to an unspecified location. The arithmetic and logical

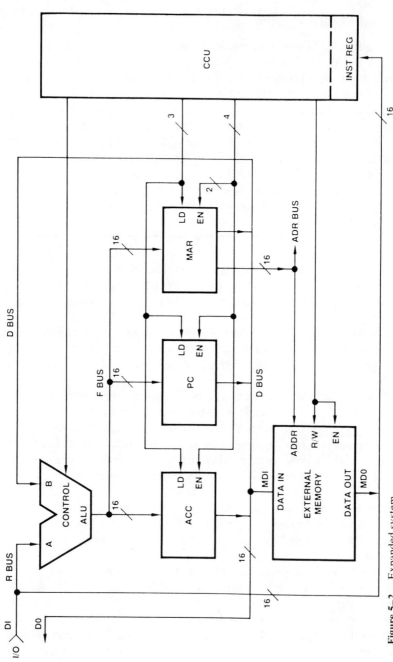

Figure 5-2. Expanded system.

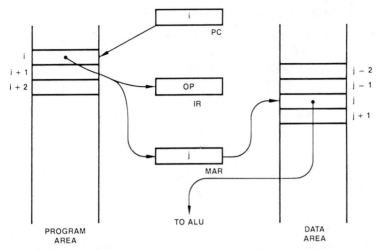

Figure 5–3.   Single address operation of SIMCOM. The PC contains the address of the instruction to be fetched. It transfers its contents to the MAR and then increments. The MAR is used to address memory. The instruction (in this example) is brought out to the instruction register (IR) and to the memory address register (MAR). The IR contains the op code to be decoded by the CCU. The MAR contains the address of the operand which must be fetched before the op code is executed.

operations and the LDA and STO operations assume that the op-address format is processed as described earlier. The JMP and JMZ assume that the PC is loaded with the address provided within the instruction.

Improving ALU Speed

Current Instruction Execution

Referring to SIMCOM as encoded so far, the number of microcycles required to perform the software operation B = A + B (where A and B are memory location) is fixed at 9.

The operations involved are given in Table 5–2. $<x>$ means contents of location, $<<x>>$ means contents of the location addressed by $<x>$, and $<>|<>$ means place left side of the equation into both locations of right side. (The PC could have been incremented as a last step in the routines.) This is suitable if all arithmetic requires memory accesses.

Scratchpad Registers

In many instances, with emphasis on the cases where a high volume of computation is performed, an arithmetic operation is performed on

Table 5–1 Basic Instruction Set

LDA, Addr.	Load accumulator with contents of address (main memory)
ADD, Addr.	Add accumulator and contents of address
SUB, Addr.	Subtract accumulator from contents of address
OR, Addr.	OR accumulator and contents of address
AND, Addr.	AND accumulator and contents of address
XOR, Addr.	Exclusive OR accumulator and contents of address
INA	Input to accumulator (from data bus)
OUT	Output from accumulator (to data bus)
JMP, Addr.	Jump to address (GO TO)
JMZ, Addr.	Jump to address IF accumulator is 0, $<ACC> = 0$
STO, Addr.	Store contents of accumulator at address (main memory)

the result of a former arithmetic operation or an operation may use the same operands as were used in a former operation. In those cases where the data is to be accessed several times or where the result of one operation is to be used several times before it is to be stored into main memory, the availability of scratchpad registers can be shown to improve the system throughput.

Table 5–2 Software Operation B = A + B (Memory Addressing)

Program Level	Machine Level	Microcode Level
B = A + B	LDA, MEMA	1. $<PC> \rightarrow <MAR> \rightarrow$ ADDR BUS $<PC> \leftarrow <PC> + 1$ $<<PC>> \rightarrow <IR> \mid <MAR>$ (dual destination)
		2. DECODE
		3. $<MAR> \rightarrow$ ADDR BUS $<<MAR>> \rightarrow <ACC>$
	ADD, MEMB	4. $<PC> \rightarrow <MAR> \rightarrow$ ADDR BUS $<PC> \leftarrow <PC> + 1$ $<<PC>> \rightarrow <IR> \mid <MAR>$
		5. DECODE
		6. $<MAR> \rightarrow$ ADDR BUS $<<MAR>> + <ACC> \rightarrow <ACC>$
	STO, MEMB	7. $<PC> \rightarrow <MAR> \rightarrow$ ADDR BUS $<PC> \leftarrow <PC> + 1$ $<<PC>> \rightarrow <IR> \mid <MAR>$
		8. DECODE $<MAR> \rightarrow$ ADDR BUS
		9. $<ACC> \rightarrow <<MAR>>$

If the operand data is already in appropriate registers, and if the result is to be kept in one of those registers, the operation

$$R_B = R_A + R_B$$

is performed with three microcycles.

To implement this, one format for register operation is

Op Code (8)	R_{Source} (4)	$R_{Destination}$ (4)

This format allows 256 different register op codes and 16 registers. This format also requires that the instruction register be as wide as the format (i.e., 16 bits in this example). (The decode of the op code would prevent the MAR being used to perform a memory access if memory addressing and register addressing are used in the same system.) The CCU controls the connection of the register addresses to the scratchpad block via a MUX.

Generalized ACC

By using a multiport scratchpad block both source registers may be accessed at once. By using the scratchpad block to replace the single register ACC, 16 different accumulators are possible. The structure is shown in Figure 5-4.

The complete microcode would be given as in Table 5–3.

If all instructions are required to be register oriented, the instruction set could look like that shown in Table 5–4. As a variation, even when any register could be used as the accumulator, some default or implied addressing instructions are desirable for code compaction. These are usually selected to be the most frequently occurring instructions such as load from memory or increment. For SIMCOM, if the R_0 register were the default ACC, the load and the store instructions would become LDR, addr. and STO, addr. As an option, both implied addressing and defined addressing versions of instructions are often included to permit the greatest power and flexibility in an instruction set.

In order to perform the register operation itself in one microcycle, the system timing must be such that the instruction cycle is long enough to allow the read register access, the ALU operation, and the write register data and address setup.

Generalized PC

Another change can be made to advantage—the PC can be moved into the scratchpad block (i.e., any register can be the PC register.)

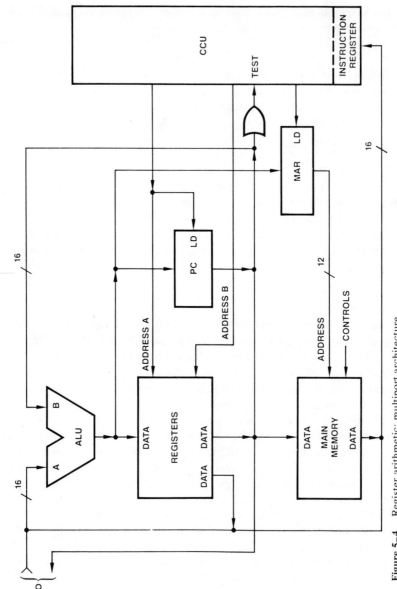

Figure 5–4.   Register arithmetic: multiport architecture.

Table 5–3   Software Operation $R_B = R_A + R_B$ (Register Addressing)

Program Level	Machine Level	Microcode Level
$R_B = R_A + R_B$	ADD, R_A, R_B	1. $<PC> \rightarrow <MAR> \rightarrow$ ADDR BUS $<PC> \leftarrow <PC> + 1$ $<<PC>> \rightarrow <IR>$ $\rightarrow <MAR>$ 2. DECODE 3. $<R_A> + <R_B> \rightarrow <R_B>$ under CCU control

This allows arithmetic operations to be performed on the program address as is required in relative addressing, for example, where the PC is added to a base register to find the actual address. Indexed addressing and various other addressing structures are now feasible using high speed register arithmetic. The resulting structure is shown in Figure 5-5.

Adding Flexibility

The scratchpad memory B port is connected to the B port of the ALU, to the main memory, and to the data output bus. The A port is connected to the A port of the ALU and also to the status-generating logic for input to the CCU. Note that either the A port or B port of the scratchpad memory could have been connected to the data output bus.

Table 5–4   SIMCOM Register Instruction Set

LDR, REG, Addr.	Load contents of main memory address into register (2 word instruction)
ADD, REG_1, REG_2	Add contents of REG_1 to REG_2, put results into REG_2
SUB, REG_1, REG_2	Subtract contents of REG_1 from REG_2, put results into REG_2
OR, REG_1, REG_2	OR REG_1 with REG_2, put results into REG_2
AND, REG_1, REG_2	AND REG_1 with REG_2, put results into REG_2
XOR, REG_1, REG_2	Exclusive OR REG_1 with REG_2, put results into REG_2
INR, REG	Input to register
OUT, REG	Output from register
JMP, REG	Jump direct to contents of register
JMZ, REG_1, REG_2	If REG_1 is zero, then jump direct to contents of REG_2
MOV, REG_1, REG_2	Move contents of REG_1 into REG_2
STO, REG, Addr.	Store contents of register at main memory address

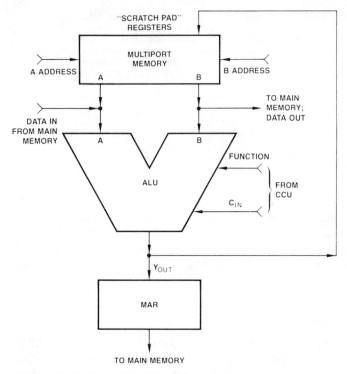

Figure 5–5. Redrawing the structure.

Input MUX A

The A port of the ALU receives input from the data input bus or the scratchpad memory A port; therefore these devices must be tristate. Assume that all input devices already are tristate. This leaves the tristate requirement for the scratchpad memory output. By adding an input MUX to the A port of the ALU and controlling this MUX from the CCU, the tristate requirement for the scratchpad A port is removed (Figure 5–6).

Output MUX

The ALU output is connected to the input port of the scratchpad and to the input of the MAR register. Improvement is possible by allowing the MAR to be loaded from either the scratchpad registers or from the ALU output and allowing the main memory input and the data output bus to share the connection. A MUX added at the output of the ALU and connected to the data output bus under control of the CCU provides this capability.

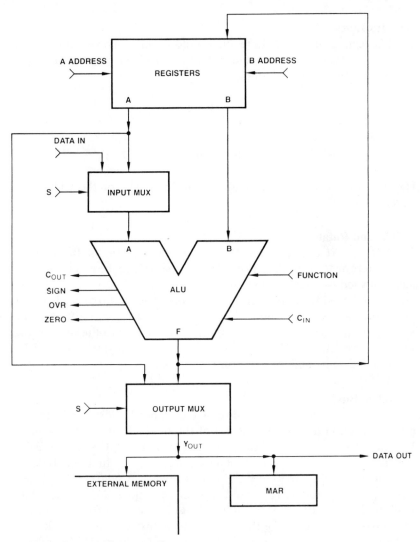

Figure 5–6.   Adding status flags.

The MAR can be loaded from the main memory by passing the data through the ALU. The MAR can also be loaded from any of the scratchpad registers for relative addressing or indexed addressing without passing through the ALU. This has advantages, in addition to the faster execution time, which will be demonstrated below. The execution time to transfer from the scratchpad register to main memory is also reduced by bypassing the ALU. (Note that in Figure 5–6 the scratchpad A port rather than the B port was used to input to the MUX.)

Status Lines

CCU testing of the ALU result should be more powerful than the $<ACC> = 0$ test. The next addition to the ALU is the provision of a number of other status outputs:

C_{out}	carry out, C_{n+4}
SIGN	C_{n+3}
OVR	$C_{n+4} \veebar C_{n+3}$
ZERO	$D_i = 0, i = 0, \ldots, n - 1$

These would be connected to the condition MUX of the CCU constructed earlier.

Shift and Rotate

While the ALU is capable of most operations, the ability to shift right or left or to rotate right or left is a desirable feature. This can be accomplished by the addition shown in Figure 5–7, where a shift register has been added at the scratchpad input. The shift register is under CCU control. External connections determine whether a shift or rotate is being performed and what bit, 0 or 1, is shifted into the high or the low order bit. A shift MUX will be needed for each side of the ALU, which will also be under CCU control.

Control Bits

Each item added which requires CCU control adds a field to the microinstruction format. The width of the field added is a function of the amount of flexibility of the device. For a shift MUX, a 2 or 3 bit field is required. The ALU so far requires a 3 bit function field, a carry-in field (or a carry-in MUX control field), A address and B address fields of 4 bits each for fixed register operations, MUX select bits to allow the A and B register addresses to be supplied from either the microinstruction register or the machine level instruction in the IR, and controls for the A port input MUX, the ALU output MUX, and the shift register. The microinstruction fields required by this version of the ALU are shown in Figure 5–8.

Double Precision

The simple system under development has no multiply or divide operations. To provide the capability for these operations, the ALU must have at least one double precision register. For the system developed so far, this is provided by adding an extension Q register and its own shift register. The ALU inputs to the Q register directly. The Q

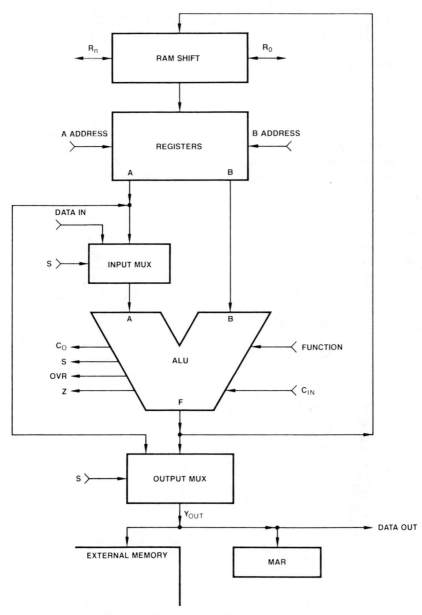

Figure 5-7. Adding the shifter at the RAM input.

shift register is connected to the output of the Q register. The Q register output also connects to the B port of the ALU. To avoid requiring a tristate register and a tristate scratchpad memory, a MUX is added to

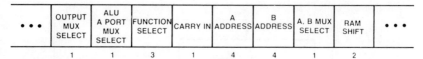

● ● ●	OUTPUT MUX SELECT	ALU A PORT MUX SELECT	FUNCTION SELECT	CARRY IN	A ADDRESS	B ADDRESS	A, B MUX SELECT	RAM SHIFT	● ● ●
	1	1	3	1	4	4	1	2	

Figure 5–8. ALU portion of the microword (simple system).

the ALU B port input and the MUX is under CCU control. External connections determine the shift or rotate operations on Q alone or Q and a scratchpad register. The addition is shown in Figure 5–9.

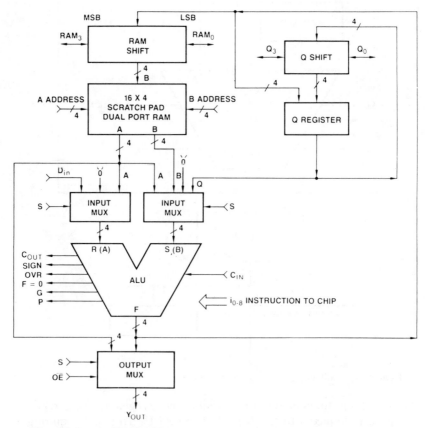

Figure 5–9. Am2901 RALU.

Additional Modifications

A few additional improvements can be made: First, adding a zero input to the ALU A and B port input MUXs allows incrementing and decrementing and PASS operations on both ports:

$$B + 0 \rightarrow B \qquad \text{PASS}$$

$$B + 0 + C_{in} \rightarrow B \qquad \text{INCR}$$

Second, adding the A port of the scratchpad to the ALU B port input MUX allows a fast multiply by 2:

$$A + A \rightarrow A \qquad \text{MULT } 2^*A$$

Third, adding an output enable control and making the ALU output MUX into a tristate MUX allows the ALU to share a bus. Finally, adding two additional status outputs, carry generate $\overline{G}$ and carry propagate $\overline{P}$, allows fast addition using carry-lookahead if the ALU is assumed to be a 4 bit wide slice. The result is shown in Figure 5–9 and is a logical block diagram of the Am2901 bit-slice RALU.

Am2901

The Am2901C is twice as fast as the original Am2901. (Each increment is used to indicate faster, more reliable, pin compatible devices.)

The microinstruction control required by the Am2901 is a 9 bit field divided into 3 bit subfields.

Source Control

The selection of the operand sources via a 3 bit subfield allows the combinations shown in Table 5–5. The combinations QQ, DD were considered to occur too seldom and 00 was considered trivial.

Table 5–5 Am2901 Source Selection

Pairing	Microcontrol Bits $I_2 I_1 I_0$ (Octal)	
AQ	0	(equivalent to BQ, QB, or QA)
AB	1	(equivalent to AA or BB)
0Q	2	(equivalent to Q0)
0B	3	(equivalent to B0)
0A	4	(equivalent to A0)
DA	5	(equivalent to DB, BD, or AD)
DQ	6	(equivalent to QD)
D0	7	(equivalent to 0D)

Function Control

The functions allowed are the simple arithmetic and logical operations. (AMD uses R and S for A and B to avoid confusion with the A and B ports of the scratchpad.) The functions selectable with a 3 bit subfield are in Table 5–6.

Destination Control

The more complex control is the destination control field. The 3-bit field must select among up, down, and no shift for the RAM shift register, choose if the scratchpad memory is to be loaded, select among up, down, and no shift of the Q shift register, choose if Q is to be loaded, and select the output MUX for ALU or scratchpad. Since some operations imply others, Table 5–7 simplifies the control selection.

Interconnection

The Am2901 is a 4 bit slice RALU intended for two's complement arithmetic and active high data. Any number of slices may be connected to construct a CPU of any multiple of 4 bits width.

Figure 5–10 shows a 12 bit CPU connected using the C_{in} and C_{out} pins in a ripple–carry configuration. Figure 5–11 shows a 16 bit CPU connected using the $\bar{G}$ and $\bar{P}$ pins of the Am2901s and an Am2902A, a carry-lookahead unit. The execution time is considerably faster using carry-lookahead. The technique of lookahead will not be discussed further.

Table 5–6 Am2901 Function Selection

Operation	Microcontrol Bits $I_5 I_4 I_3$ (Octal)	
R + S	0	
S − R	1	
R − S	2	
R $\vee$ S	3	
R $\wedge$ S	4	
$\bar{R} \wedge$ S	5	
R $\forall$ S	6	Exclusive or
R $\equiv$ S	7	Identity

Table 5-7   Am2901 Destination Control

	Microcode				RAM Function		Q-REG. Function		Y	RAM Shifter		Q Shifter	
Mnemonic	I_8	I_7	I_6	Octal Code	Shift	Load	Shift	Load	Output	RAM_0	RAM_3	Q_0	Q_3
OREG	L	L	L	0	X	None	None	F→Q	F	X	X	X	X
NOP	L	L	H	1	X	None	X	None	F	X	X	X	X
RAMA	L	H	L	2	None	F→B	X	None	A	X	X	X	X
RAMF	L	H	H	3	None	F→B	X	None	F	X	X	X	X
RAMQD	H	L	L	4	Down	F/2→B	Down	Q/2→Q	F	F_0	IN_3	Q_0	IN_3
RAMD	H	L	H	5	Down	F/2→B	X	None	F	F_0	IN_3	Q_0	X
RAMQU	H	H	L	6	Up	2F→B	Up	2Q→Q	F	IN_0	F_3	IN_0	Q_3
RAMU	H	H	H	7	Up	2F→B	X	None	F	IN_0	F_3	X	Q_3

X, "don't care." Electrically, the shift pin is a TTL input internally connected to a three-state output which is in the high-impedance state. B, register addressed by B inputs. Up is toward MSB, Down is toward LSB.

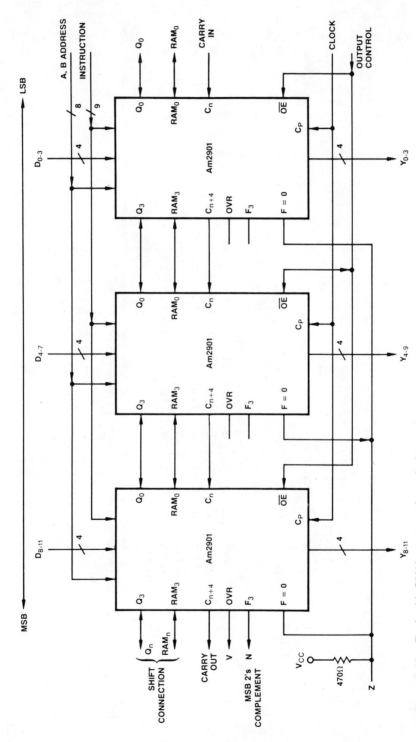

Figure 5–10. Twelve-bit CPU interconnections (ripple carry).

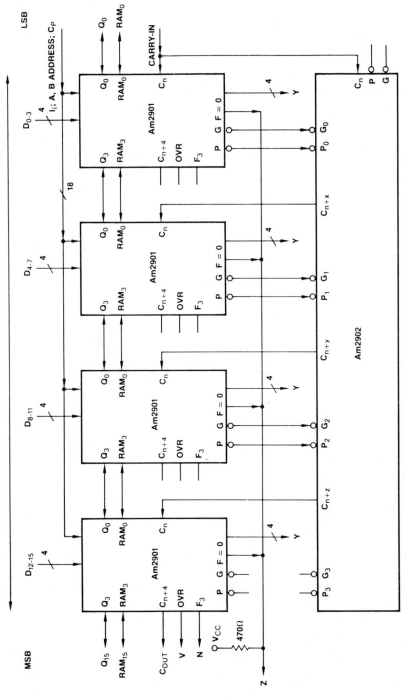

Figure 5–11. Sixteen-bit CPU interconnections (carry-lookahead).

The ALU
and Basic
Arithmetic

Further Enhancements

If we alter the Am2901 architecture as follows then we have the Am2903 or the AMD Superslice™ RALU shown in Figure 6-1:

1. add connections and controls to allow for vertical expansion of the scratchpad registers;

2. rearrange the Q shift and Q registers so that the ALU loads into the Q shift register directly;

3. move the RAM shift to the ALU output;

4. allow data to be input on the ALU B port instead of the A port;

5. allow data to be output from the B port of the scratchpad, which requires a tristate buffering of that port;

6. allow the data to be input directly into the scratchpad memory, bypassing the ALU;

7. share the $\overline{G}$ and $\overline{P}$ pins with SIGN and OVR;

8. enable the device to know if it is the most, least, or middle significant slice, to allow arithmetic shifting; and

9. increase the possible functions which the ALU can perform.

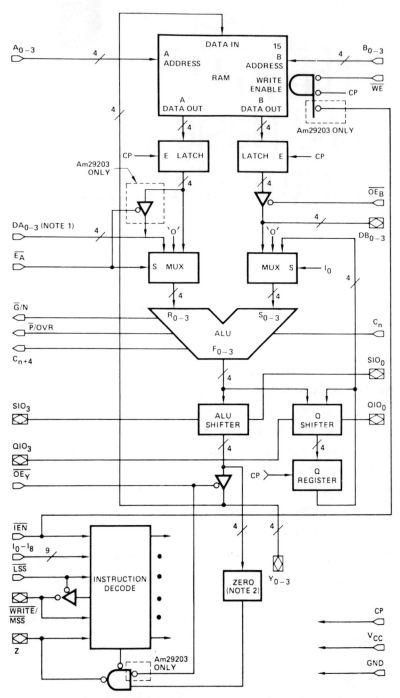

Notes: 1. DA_{0-3} is input only on Am2903, but is I/O port on Am29203.
2. On Am29203, zero logic is connected to Y, after the OE_Y buffer.

Figure 6–1. Am2903 RALU.

In addition to the 9 bit instruction input, various other input controls are needed:

$\overline{OE}_Y$	Output enable for the bidirectional Y output
$\overline{OE}_B$	Output enable for the bidirectional DB output
$\overline{E}_A$	MUX select control for the ALU A port input
I_0	One of the instruction lines—MUX select control for the ALU B port input
$\overline{W}_E$	Write enable for the scratchpad, used for expanded memory (all slices are tied to $\overline{WRITE/MSS}$ of least significant slice)
$\overline{LSS}$	LOW = least significant slice and enables $\overline{WRITE}$ as output; HIGH = $\overline{WRITE}$ is an input
$\overline{WRITE}$	As input, HIGH = intermediate slice and LOW = most significant slice
I_{EN}	Instruction enable
C_N	Carry in

There are three ways to input or output data:

Y_{0-3}	Data I/O pins
D_{0-3}	Data I/O pins (D_A port or D_B port)

There are three status pins:

$\overline{G}$ and SIGN	Carry generate or Y_{n+3}
P and OVR	Carry propagate or $C_{n+4} \forall C_{n+3}$
C_{n+4}	Carry out

The most significant slice (MSS) produces the SIGN and OVR signals and IS and LSS devices produce $\overline{P}$ and $\overline{G}$. A 16 bit carry-lookahead RALU is shown in Figure 6–2.

Finally, there are the scratchpad pins:

$$\left.\begin{array}{l} A_{0-3} \\ \\ B_{0-3} \end{array}\right\} \text{Address select}$$

The Am2903 is more powerful than the Am2901. It has a richer instruction set, including nine special functions which use user-unaccessible internal controls to facilitate operations such as two's complement multiply, sign extend, and normalization. It can be used with an expanded scratchpad memory so that the RALU is no longer limited to 16 registers. The ability to identify a slice as to its significance contributes to the instructional power available. The Am29203 will feature additional special instructions (BCD arithmetic).

Like the Am2900 family in general, the Am2903 is a low power Schottky device with tristate outputs. The Am2903 is in a 48 pin package. The Am2903A and the Am29203 are ECL internal and TTL external for higher speeds.

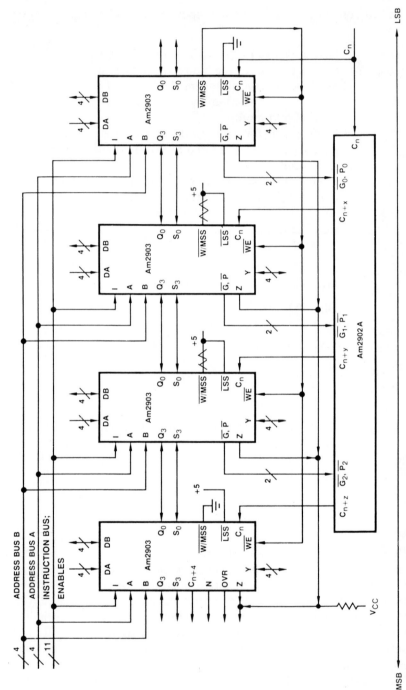

Figure 6–2.   Sixteen-bit CPU with carry-lookahead.

Instruction Fields

The basic 9 bit instruction field is broken up into subfields differently from the Am2901: I_{5-8} identify the destination, shifting, etc., I_{1-4} identify the ALU function, and I_0 is a MUX select. I_0 normally appears with $\overline{E}_A$ and $\overline{OE}_B$ as a 3 bit source select control field.

Instruction Set Extensions

The basic arithmetic and logic function set of the Am2903 has several extensions to that of the Am2901, including all HIGH and all LOW and the logical NAND and NOR functions (Table 6-1).

Shifting

There are two types of shifting possible owing to the identification of the significance of the slices. The logical shift shifts through all bit positions. The arithmetic shift shifts around the most significant bit

Table 6-1   Am2903 ALU Functions*

I_4	I_3	I_2	I_1	Hex Code	ALU Functions*
L	L	L	L	0	$I_0 = $ L, special functions
					$I_0 = $ H, $F_i = $ HIGH
L	L	L	H	1	$F = S - R - 1 + C_n$
L	L	H	L	2	$F = R - S - 1 + C_n$
L	L	H	H	3	$F = R + S = C_n$
L	H	L	L	4	$F = S + C_n$
L	H	L	H	5	$F = \overline{S} + C_n$
L	H	H	L	6	$F = R + C_n$
L	H	H	H	7	$F = \overline{R} + C_n$
H	L	L	L	8	$F_i = $ LOW
H	L	L	H	9	$F_i = \overline{R}_i$ AND S_i
H	L	H	L	A	$F_i = R_i$ exclusive NOR S_i
H	L	H	H	B	$F_i = R_i$ exclusive OR S_i
H	H	L	L	C	$F_i = R_i$ AND S_i
H	H	L	H	D	$F_i = R_i$ NOR S_i
H	H	H	L	E	$F_i = R_i$ NAND S_i
H	H	H	H	F	$F_i = R_i$ OR S_i

*6, 7, 8 require $I_0 = $ LOW

L, LOW; H, HIGH; i = 0–3.

position, i.e., the sign is undisturbed. The Am2903 data sheet provides a detailed table for the destination–shift control. Note that the source–ALU and destination control tables are valid only if

$$(I_0 + I_1 + I_2 + I_3 + I_4)I_{EN} = 1$$

For the case

$$\overline{I}_0\,\overline{I}_1\,\overline{I}_2\,\overline{I}_3\,\overline{I}_4\,\overline{I}_{EN} = 1$$

the special functions override the normal chip operations, with I_{5-8} as the function select control field.

Three-Address Operation

The Am2903 may be used to perform a three-address operation. The given A-B addresses are used as the source addresses and a third address used as the destination. The second and third addresses are input to a MUX whose selection is under clock control such that the B address is stable for the read and the C address is stable for the write. The third address must be in a register. The actual WRITE takes place on the rising edge of the clock. See the Am2903 data sheet for control details.

Sample Operations

Some operations will be examined for the two RALU slices, the Am2901 and Am2903.

Increment

It is desired to increment a register and *at the same time* output its original value:

$$R'_A \leftarrow R_A + 1; \quad R_A \rightarrow out$$

Assume that the register is R_{15} and that it has been previously loaded with a value.

Am2901 Version

The Am2901 microcontrols are derived by examining each subfield table. The A and B addresses will both be F_{16}. The only way to output from the scratchpad is to select A with the output MUX. This leaves the B,0 pair as the source control; therefore $I_2I_1I_0$ is set at 3_8. The ALU function is add or increment; therefore $I_5I_4I_3$ is set to 0_8 and C_N set to 1. The result of the ADD is to be passed around from the ALU output F to the RAM shift register and then to the scratchpad memory, to R_{15}. This is the destination control F→B, A→Y; therefore $I_8I_7I_6$ is set at 2_8. The complete microword for the Am2901 is

I_8	I_7	I_6	I_5	I_4	I_3	I_2	I_1	I_0	C_N	A_3	A_2	A_1	A_0	B_3	B_2	B_1	B_0
0	1	0	0	0	0	0	1	1	1	1	1	1	1	1	1	1	1

The data flow is given in Figure 6–3.

Am2903 Version

The same problem approach is used with the Am2903. The only way to output directly from the scratchpad is via the DB_{out} path, which requires $\overline{OE}_B$ be held LOW. The ALU will add A + 0; therefore $I_4I_3I_2I_1$ will be set to 6_{16}, C_{in} set to 1, and I_0 set to 0. The A port input MUX select $\overline{E}_A$ is set LOW. The A and B addresses are set to F_{16}, assuming R_{15} is in use. Since Y will be used to input back into the scratchpad, $\overline{OE}_Y$ = LOW and $\overline{WE}$ will be driven by $\overline{WRITE/MSS}$. The complete microword for the Am2903 is

I_8	I_7	I_0	I_5	I_4	I_3	I_2	I_1	$\overline{E}_A$	I_0	$\overline{OE}_BC_N$
1	1	1	1	0	0	1	1	0	0	0 1

OE_Y	A_3	A_2	A_1	A_0	B_3	B_2	B_1	B_0
0	1	1	1	1	1	1	1	1

The data flow is given in Figure 6–4.

Byte Swap

A 16-bit byte swap exchanges bits B_{15}–B_8 with B_7–B_0 in order and vice versa:

Assume a 16 bit ALU (4 slices) and that the register in question is R_{15}.

Am2901 Version

The Am2901 microcode solution can be constructed by taking advantage of the fact that a shift up is equivalent to multiplying by 2. If the result of an add of R_{15} + R_{15} is shifted (prior to storing the result) into R_{15}, the effect is a 2-bit rotate, assuming that (1) the high order

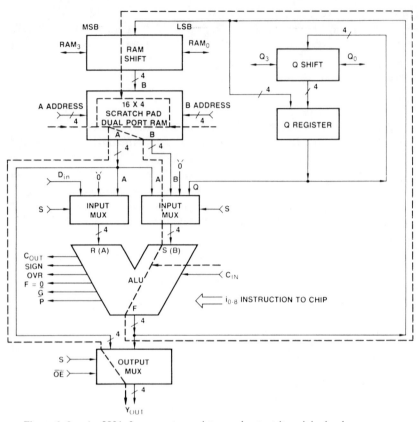

Figure 6–3. Am2901: Increment a register *and* output its original value.

input/output of the RAM shift is connected to the low order input/output of the RAM and (2) the carry out C_{n+4} is connected to the carry in C_{in}. Since we are selecting source operands as A, B, adding, and shifting, $2F{\rightarrow}B$; the microword is

$$
\begin{array}{ccc|cccccc|c|cccc|cccc}
I_8 & I_7 & I_6 & I_5 & I_4 & I_3 & I_2 & I_1 & I_0 & C_{in} & A_3 & A_2 & A_1 & A_0 & B_3 & B_2 & B_1 & B_0 \\
1 & 1 & 1 & 0 & 0 & 0 & 0 & 0 & 1 & C_{out} & 1 & 1 & 1 & 1 & 1 & 1 & 1 & 1
\end{array}
$$

The microinstruction must be repeated four times to cause an 8-bit rotate, for a total timing of four microcycles of approximately 165 ns worst case minimum (dependent upon the actual hardware).

Am2903 Version

The Am2903 microcode solution is approached the same way. The S shift is connected for rotate as was the RAM shift of the Am2901, the carry out is input to the carry in, and an add is performed. The complete microword is

$$
\begin{array}{cccc|cccc|cccc}
I_8 & I_7 & I_6 & I_5 & I_4 & I_3 & I_2 & I_1 & E_A & I_0 & E_B & C_n \\
1 & 0 & 0 & 1 & 0 & 0 & 1 & 1 & 0 & 0 & 0 & C_{out}
\end{array}
$$

$$
\begin{array}{ccccc|cccc}
OE_Y & A_3 & A_2 & A_1 & A_0 & B_3 & B_2 & B_1 & B_0 \\
0 & 1 & 1 & 1 & 1 & 1 & 1 & 1 & 1
\end{array}
$$

Am2901 Hardware Version

The byte-swap operation can be performed faster using additional (such as Am25LS240/244) tristate buffers (select noninverting). The Am2901 Y outputs are gated out to the buffers, which in turn input to the appropriate D_A inputs of another Am2901. The operation performed by the Am2901 in this case is to output from the scratchpad, $Y \rightarrow A$, and to pass the D_A input thru the ALU and back into the scratchpad memory, $F \rightarrow B$. The additional hardware allows the byte swap to be done in one microcycle. The microword is

$$
\begin{array}{ccc|ccc|ccc|c}
I_8 & I_7 & I_6 & I_5 & I_4 & I_3 & I_2 & I_1 & I_0 & C_{in} \\
0 & 1 & 0 & 0 & 0 & 0 & 1 & 1 & 1 & 0
\end{array} \cdots
$$

Am2903 Hardware Version

There are two ways to perform a hardware-assisted byte swap using the Am2903 and the Am25LS240/244 buffers. One approach is to use the D_B as the output to the buffers and to use D_A as the input point. This is the relatively slower approach, since the D_A input passes the data through the ALU and back to the scratchpad.

The other approach uses the Y port as the data input, which provides a data path directly into the scratchpad. This method avoids the propagation delay of the ALU, shift register, tristate buffer, and input MUX. The microwords are

$$
\begin{array}{c|cccc|cccc|cc|cc|cc}
 & I_8 & I_7 & I_6 & I_5 & I_4 & I_3 & I_2 & I_1 & \overline{E}_A & I_0 & \overline{OE}_B & C_n & \overline{OE}_Y & N_E \\
D_A & 1 & 1 & 1 & 1 & 0 & 0 & 1 & 1 & 1 & 0 & 0 & 0 & 0 & 0 \ldots \\
Y & 1 & 1 & 1 & 1 & X & X & X & X & X & X & 0 & X & 1 & 0
\end{array}
$$

The basic difference is the $\overline{OE}_Y$ control.

Arithmetic—General

The Am2901 and Am2903 perform two's complement arithmetic. Two's complement notation is a weighted binary code, where the sign

bit (most significant bit) has a negative weight. For example, for an
8 bit system $37_{10} = (00100101)_2$, computed as

$$-0*2^7 + 0*2^6 + 1*2^5 + 0*2^4\ 0*2^3 + 0*2^2 + 0*2^1 + 1*2^0$$
$$= 32 + 4 + 1$$
$$= 37_{10}$$

For the same system, $-37_{10} = (11011011)_2$ is computed as

$$-1*2^7 + 1*2^6 + 0*2^5 + 1*2^4 + 1*2^3 + 0*2^2 + 1*2^1 + 1*2^0$$
$$= -128 + 64 + 16 + 8 + 2 + 1$$
$$= -37_{10}$$

The negative number encoding can be formed by logically comple-
menting all bits and adding 1 to the encoding of the positive number.

The advantage of the two's complement number system is that there
is a *single zero*. The numbers are normally considered to be binary
fractions, so that a positive number is less than 1 and a negative
number is greater than 1.

Addition

Addition is performed as a straightforward binary addition, with the
sign of the result dependent on the signs of the operands.

For two positive numbers the sign is positive, and for two negative
numbers it is negative. A check should *always* be made for overflow,
which is possible when the sums of the magnitudes exceed 1. The
Am2901 and Am2903 both provide an overflow pin

$$OVR = C_{n+4} \veebar C_{n+3}$$

to allow status checking.

When the two operands have opposite signs, the sign of the result is
always the sign of the larger.

Subtraction

Subtraction is processed in the same manner as addition, i.e., complement the subtrahend and add. Both the Am2901 and Am2903 provide two subtraction operations, $A-B$ and $B-A$.

Multiplication

The most difficult of the arithmetic operations so far is multiplication.

Unsigned Binary

To perform $B \times A$ in two's complement, where the numbers are
either both unsigned or both positive, the procedure is the same as for
binary multiplication. The multiplier is examined bit by bit right to left
(least significant to most significant bit) to determine if the multiplicand
is to be added to the partial result. If so, the multiplicand is aligned so

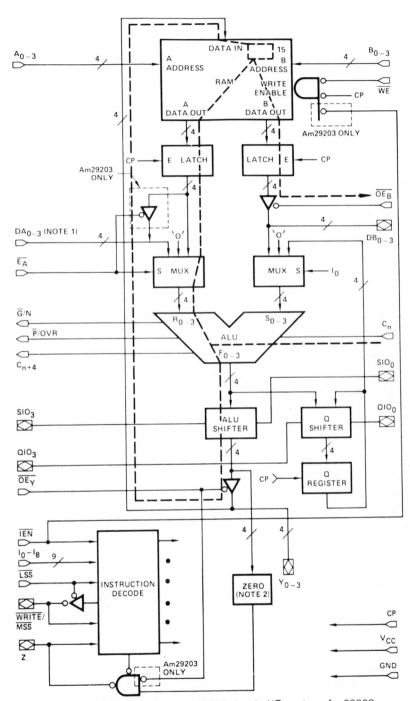

Notes: 1. DA_{0-3} is input only on Am2903, but is I/O port on Am29203.
   2. On Am29203, zero logic is connected to Y, after the OE_Y buffer.

Figure 6–4.   Am2903: Increment a register and output its original value.

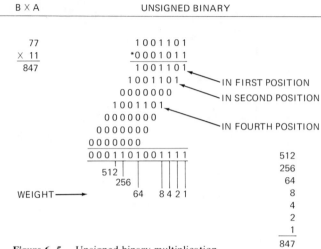

B X A   UNSIGNED BINARY

```
        77                        1 0 0 1 1 0 1
      X 11                       *0 0 0 1 0 1 1
       847                        1 0 0 1 1 0 1
                                  1 0 0 1 1 0 1          IN FIRST POSITION
                                  0 0 0 0 0 0 0          IN SECOND POSITION
                                1 0 0 1 1 0 1
                                0 0 0 0 0 0 0
                                0 0 0 0 0 0 0            IN FOURTH POSITION
                              0 0 0 0 0 0 0
                              0 0 0 1 1 0 1 0 0 1 1 1 1              512
                                 512                                256
                                    256                             64
    WEIGHT                              64    8 4 2 1               8
                                                                    4
                                                                    2
                                                                    1
                                                                   847
```

Figure 6–5.   Unsigned binary multiplication.

that the least significant bit of the multiplicand is under the multiplier bit's position, as shown in Figure 6–5.

If the bit is 1, add the multiplicand; if the bit is 0, add zero. The result of an N bit multiply is at most $2N$ bits.

Multiplicand Negative

When the multiplicand is negative, $B*(-A)$, sign extension of the multiplicand is used to form the first partial product, maintaining the $2n$ length of the magnitude. Each time the multiplicand is added, the sign extension form is used. The sign of the multiplicand is the sign of the result.

Multiplier Negative

When the multiplier is negative, $(-B)*A$, the multiplication proceeds as for the unsigned or both-positive case, except that at the end the two's complement of A, the multiplicand, is added aligned on the binary points and *not* by placing the least significant bit of A under the sign bit of B, the multiplier.

Both Negative

Where both numbers are negative, the multiplicand is sign extended and added as for the multiplicand-negative algorithm. At the end, the two's complement of the multiplicand is added, properly aligned as for the multiplier-negative algorithm.

Result

The point of reviewing the various cases was to produce a common algorithm (method I, Flores, *Computer Arithmetic*): (1) the leftmost bits are a function of the sign of the multiplicand; (2) partial product addition is required with alignment; and (3) the two's complement of the multiplicand is added at the end *if* the sign of the multiplier is negative.

Multiplication with the Am2901

To implement the above algorithm using the Am2901, the bits of the multiplier need to be examined one at a time. To perform the addition, shifting down is necessary to maintain alignment. To conditionally add the multiplicand or 0, control of the source–operand pair (A,B) or (A,0) is required and a method of conditional subtraction is needed.

The functional diagram of the multiply operation is given in Figure 6–6. The actual schematic of a 16 bit Am2901 ALU is shown in Figure 6–7.

The additional hardware provides the following connections:

1. When Q is loaded and after each instance when it is shifted, Q_0 is inverted and connected to a MUX which is controlled from the CCU. Under multiply the MUX selects Q_0; under normal operation the MUX selects I_1. Q_0 operates to control the source operands so that

Q_0	$\bar{Q}_0$	Source Pair
0	1	B + 0
1	0	B + A

2. When R_B is shifted down (R_B is *any* scratchpad register), R_{B_0} is shifted into Q_3 of the most significant slice.

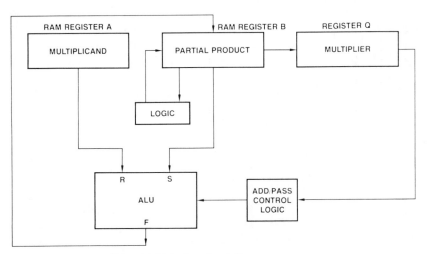

Figure 6–6.   Am2901A Multiply functional diagram.

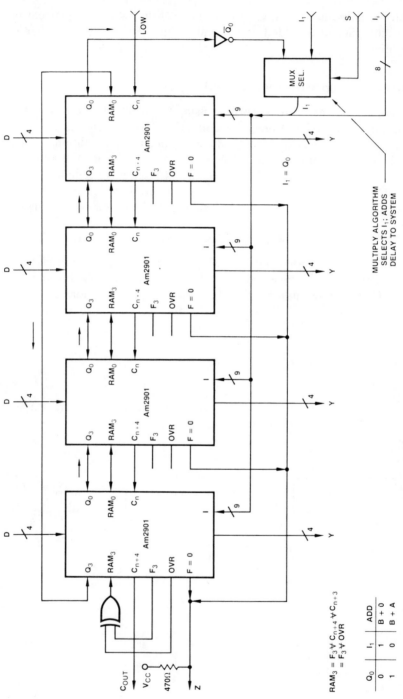

Figure 6–7. Specific interconnections for 16-bit multiply—ripple carry.

3. When R_B is shifted down SIGN $\forall$ OVR is shifted into RB_3 of the most significant slice. This is equivalent to

$$RB_3 = F_3 \forall C_{n+4} \forall C_{n+3}$$

The Algorithm

The microcode algorithm is as follows:

Clear R_B	$R_B \leftarrow 0$
Load multiplicand into R_A	$R_A \leftarrow$ multiplicand
Load multiplier into Q	$Q \leftarrow$ multiplier (Q_0 can be sensed)

If not done, add, then
    shift Q down and
    shift R_B down
	If $Q_0 = 0$, $R_B \leftarrow (R_B + 0)/2$; $Q \leftarrow Q/2$
	If $Q_0 + 1$, $R_B \leftarrow (R_B + R_A)/2$; $Q \leftarrow Q/2$
	Repeat loop until counter $= 0$

If done, add, then
    shift Q down and
    shift R_B down
	If $Q_0 = 0$, $R_B \leftarrow R_B/2$; $Q \leftarrow Q/2$
	If $Q_0 = 1$, $R_B \leftarrow (R_B - R_A)/2$; $Q \leftarrow Q/2$

The result is across registers R_B and Q, and the result is sign extended to produce the proper number of bits so that multiplication with any two 8-bit two's complement numbers always produces a 16-bit result.

A sample 8×8 bit multiply is shown in Figures 6–8 and 6–9. Figure 6–9 shows the step-by-step walkthrough of the problem. Sample microcode is given in the Am2900 Family Data Book and the 2900 Family Study Guide.

Am2903 Multiply

Unsigned Multiply

The Am2903 has unsigned multiplication implemented as one of its special functions. To perform multiplication, zero out the RAM register which, with Q, will contain the final result. If it is not already present,

```
    1 . 1 0 0 1 1 0 1              - 51
    1 . 0 0 0 1 0 1 1             -117
1 | 1 1 1 1 1 1 1 1 0 0 1 1 0 1 |  + 5967
1 | 1 1 1 1 1 1 0 0 1 1 0 1 | 0
0 | 0 0 0 0 0 0 0 0 0 0 0 0 | 0 0
1 | 1 1 1 1 0 0 1 1 0 1 | 0 0 0
0 | 0 0 0 0 0 0 0 0 0 | 0 0 0 0
0 | 0 0 0 0 0 0 0 0 | 0 0 0 0 0
0 | 0 0 0 0 0 0 0 | 0 0 0 0 0 0
1 | 1 1 1 1 0 1 1 1 0 0 1 1 1 1
0 | 0 1 1 0 0 1 1    ◄——————— "CORRECTION"
0 | 0 1 0 1 1 1 0 1 0 0 1 1 1 1 ◄——— RESULT
```

Figure 6–8. Example: 8 × 8-bit multiply two's complement ($B = -b$, $A = -a$).

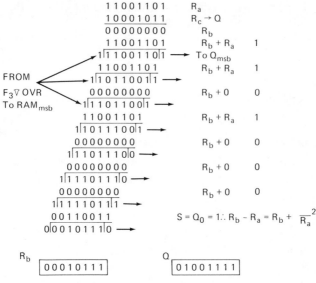

Figure 6–9. Walking through the Am2901A algorithm. The Am2901A algorithm takes advantage of added hardware to eliminate conditional jumps and therefore improve speed and reduce microcode.

load the multiplicand into another RAM register. Load the multiplier into the Q register. The shift connection should tie the LSB (least significant bit) of the RAM register (S_0) to the MSB (most significant bit) of the Q register (Q_3) of the most significant slice.

The actual microcode is two microwords—(1) load the Am2910 counter with the number of bits minus 1 (for 16×16, load with 15) and place the multiplier into Q, and (2) use RPCT for the Am2910 to repeat the actual multiply operation.

Two's Complement Multiply

The Am2903 has two other special functions which enable multiplication of a signed number. Two's complement multiply requires three microwords for any width multiplication.

The same initialization is required, with the multiplier being placed into the Q register. The counter in this case is loaded with the number of bits minus 2 (for 16×16, load with 14). The repeat loop instruction is the same as before. The added step is effectively the sign bit "correction" which was the last step in the Am2901 algorithm. The required interconnect of the slices is the same as before, with the addition of the Z status line tied to C_{in}.

7

Tying
the System
Together

The two basic building blocks of a general 16 bit system—the CCU, including the firmware interrupt controller, and the RALU—have been defined in previous chapters. Various other devices are available in the Am2900 family to complete the basic CPU that has been used throughout the text.

Expanded Memory for the Am2903

The Am2903 is designed to be interconnected to the Am29705, via decoders, in order to expand the basic 16×4 scratchpad memory. The Am29705 is a true two-port 16×4 RAM memory which can operate identically to the Am2903's own scratchpad. A logic diagram of the Am29705 is given in Figure 7-1. (The Am29203 uses the Am29707.)

By expanding the A,B addresses, scratchpad memory may be added in increments of 16 registers of the equivalent width of the ALU. An expanded memory interconnect diagram is shown in Figure 7-2 (taken from the AMD data sheet).

MUX Requirements

In the course of examining the various arithmetic and shifting algorithms that any given system is to perform, including those few examined in this text, the designer will find it necessary to be able to vary (1)

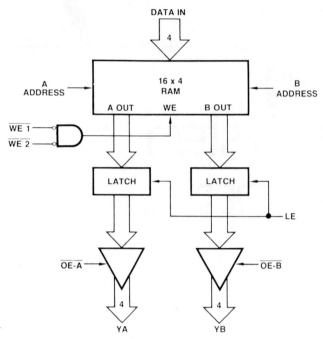

Figure 7–1. Am29705 block diagram.

the way that the RALU RAM and Q shifters interconnect, (2) the value of carry in, (3) and the source of the carry out status bit.

The carry in bit could be (1) from a field in the CCU, (2) from the ALU C_{out} (for rotate-by-add or for multiple word precision algorithms), or (3) from the ALU Z status line (for the Am2903 multiply), for example. The carry out bit could be sourced from (1) the C_{n+4} of the RALU or (2) the RAM_3 (or S_3) output of the RAM shifter.

The shift and the rotate interconnections are determined by the particular variations which any given design is to implement. RAM_0 (Am2901) or S_0 (Am2903) might require connection to C_{out}, RAM_3 (S_3), Q_3 (extension register shifter), and ground or Vcc or both. Q_0 might require a similar flexibility of connection. RAM_3 (S_3) and Q_3 would require complementary connection capability.

In each of these cases, the most obvious solution has been to employ multiplexers with the microinstruction supplying the appropriate selection for any desired connectivity pattern. The Am2904 is designed to replace the carry in MUX, the carry out MUX, the RAM_0 and RAM_3 MUXs, and the Q_0 and Q_3 MUXs. The Am2904 was developed to reduce the required SSI and MSI support which occurs in typical CPU designs.

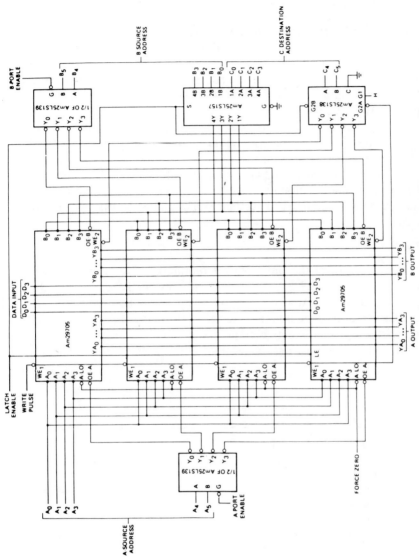

Figure 7-2. Three-address 64 by 4-bit three-address memory. Data is read from the A address to the YA outputs and from the B address to the YB outputs while the latch enable is HIGH. When the latch enable goes LOW, the YA and YB data are held in the internal latches, and the RAM B address is switched to the C-destination address lines. A write pulse will then deposit the input data into the location selected by the C address.

Status Register

In the preferred architecture, the one being emphasized throughout this text, a status register is used to hold the status produced by the previous microinstruction (such as the ALU status outputs) for use in determining the next microinstruction address ("branch on result of previous"). The status outputs of the RALU as well as certain other condition MUX inputs are considered to be microlevel status inputs. A sophisticated architecture may also have machine level status, those bits to be tested by the machine level instructions. A machine level status register is necessary in this case, and it must be settable at the individual bit level. The Am2904 includes both the microlevel and the macro or machine level status registers and provides the bit set and certain testing capabilities to further reduce the SSI-MSI support required.

Am2904

Figure 7–3 diagrams the interconnect required between the Am2904 and an array of Am2903s. A similar interconnect is required if the ALU is formed from Am2901s. Figure 7–4 presents the block diagram of the CPU that has been under discussion. It includes the IR (instruction register) connected between the system data bus and the mapping PROM and also shows its connection to the A,B address selection

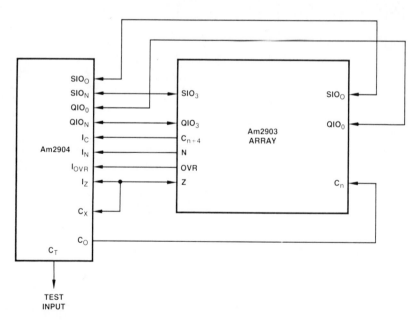

Figure 7–3.   Full interconnection of Am2904–Am2903.

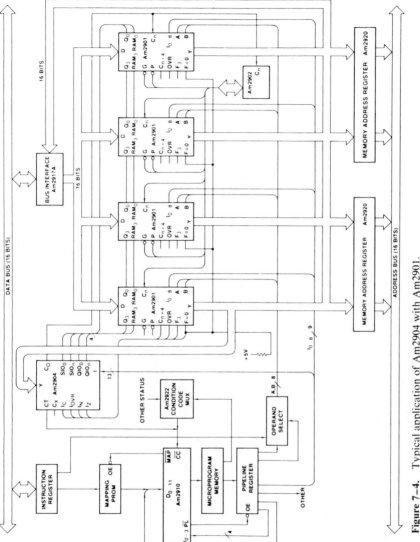

Figure 7–4. Typical application of Am2904 with Am2901.

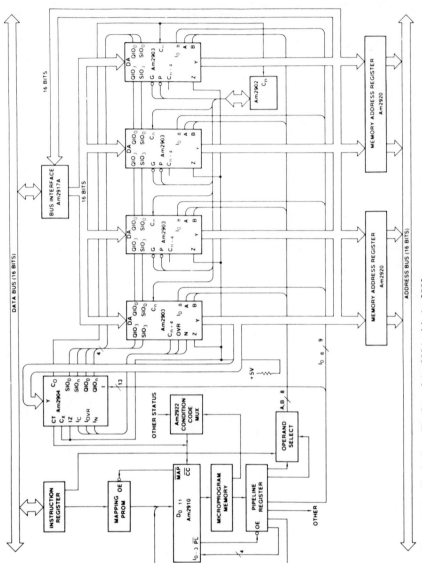

Figure 7–5.   Typical application of Am2904 with Am2903.

MUX. The mapping PROM decodes the op code and supplies an address out on tristate lines to the microprogram sequencer, an Am2910. The Am2910 supplies the microprogram address to be fetched to the microprogram memory and supplies, in this case, output enables to the mapping PROM and the pipeline register. The Am2910 receives (1) a 4 bit instruction out of the pipeline register, (2) an address into its D_i inputs (the source of the address selected by the decode of the instruction received), and (3) a condition code input on its $\overline{CC}$ line.

The $\overline{CC}$ line is connected to a condition code MUX, an Am2922 in this case, which is a registered MUX—i.e., it latches the selection code sent to it and therefore is not connected to a pipeline register. It also has polarity control. The $\overline{CC}$ line is attached to the CT output of the Am2904.

The pipeline register is sufficiently wide to contain all of the microinstruction fields in a horizontal format. In a typical system this can vary between 32 and 128 bits. The HEX-29, a generalized register architecture 16 bit CPU, has a 64 bit microword, with one field with overlay, The SUPER-16, also a 16 bit system, but with instruction-fetch overlap and certain I/O features which allow it to have a machine instruction execute time of 200 ns, has a 96 bit microword.

The Am2904 is connected to the RALU status outputs and to the most significant and least significant RAM and Q outputs. It is connected to the system data bus so that the machine level status bits can be read from or written into the status register.

The ALU consists of four Am2901 RALUs and an Am2902 carry-lookahead chip. The DA_i inputs are connected to the system data bus through a bus interface device. The Y_i outputs are also connected to the bus interface and are connected to the MAR register. The MAR register is connected to the system address bus. The A and B address lines are sourced either from the IR, for register instructions, or from the pipeline register, for implied register addressing, as selected by the microinstruction via the operand select MUX.

Figure 7–5 shows the same architecture is implemented using the Am2903 RALU rather than the Am2901.

Glossary

ACC	accumulator register
ALU	arithmetic logic unit
CC	condition code test input on Am2910
CCU	computer control unit—contains ROM or PROM or WCS; the microsequencer; the IR; the pipeline (microinstruction) register; condition code mux
C_f	minimum cycle width
C_p, CLK	clock signal (rising edge)
C_p	microcycle width; also used as clock signal (time between two rising edges C_p)
CPU	central processing unit
cycle time	when microprogramming, usually refers to one clock cycle; one microcycle or clock cycle being required to execute one microinstruction where a microinstruction is equivalent to a microstep
DIP	dual in-line pin package (other packages exist but are not as common)
DMA	direct memory access
EPROM	erasable PROM
firmware	program which controls the system; usually stored in PROM/ROM memory but not restricted to read-only memory

141

FIS	fixed instruction set
FPLA	field programmable logic delay
Hex	hexadecimal
I/O	input/output
IR	instruction register
LIFO	last in, first out
LSB	least significant bit
LSI	large scale integration (200–1000 gates per package)
LSS	least significant slice
macroinstruction	a machine level instruction
MAR	memory (main memory) address register
microinstruction	instruction which actually controls the hardware activity
microprocessor	1 chip containing control logic, registers, and ALU
microprogrammable	user may change the control program
microprogrammed	user may not change the control program
microroutine	sufficient microinstructions to execute one machine level instruction
MOS	metal oxide–silicon technology
MSB	most significant bit
MSI	medium scale integration
MSS	most significant slice
MUX	multiplexer, a select-one-of-n device
op code	part of machine level instruction which specifies function to be performed
operand	data elements which will be operated on
PC	program counter (main memory; machine programmed)
μPC	microprogram counter register; register which contains address of next microinstruction to be executed
pc board	printed circuit board
PCB	printed circuit board
PLA	programmable logic array
PROM	programmable read-only memory (user programmed) [used in text also to represent EPROMs and other variations of the basic PROM concept]
RALU	ALU with registers (scratchpad)
RAM	read and write memory
ROM	read-only memory (factory programmed)
scratchpad registers	local storage for user; system programs
SSI	small scale integration
$t_{\text{ALU execution}}$	maximum delay of AWU from instruction lines stable to ALU output useable

$t_{\text{counter clock to output}}$	maximum delay clock edge received by counter until output useable
t_i	worst case, maximum value of time t_i
t_i	worst case, minimum value of time t_i
$t_{\text{pipeline clock to output}}$	maximum delay clock edge received by counter until output usable
$t_{\text{PROM read access}}$	maximum time delay from address lines stable until PROM output stable
TOS	top of the stack
TTL	transistor-transistor logic
VLSI	very large scale integration (>1000 gates per package)
WCS	writable control store; control memory built from read-write-memory and therefore alterable (for microprogrammable systems)

Index